Praise for *Don't Stop the Career Clock*

"We may not be getting any younger, but with *Don't Stop the Career Clock* we are sure to get smarter (and think younger) with regard to our career and possible changes."

> David P. Helfand, Ph.D.
> Professor, Northeastern Illinois University
> Author of *Career Change*

"This book is essential reading for all successful people who plan to extend their productivity well beyond any sort of 'normal' retirement age."

> G. Dulany Howland, CFP
> President, G. Dulany Howland Advisory Corporation

"Helen Harkness is a true visionary, backed up with her extensive experience with people in transition. Her books have empowered me to boldly search out my own way, balancing my personal and career life to create my own nontraditional lifestyle. This is a must-read for anyone who would choose to put more gold in his or her golden years."

> Ron Watson, Real Estate Entrepreneur/Investor

"Helen Harkness presents new possibilities for careers in lieu of retirement. Breaking old models of a time-on-your-hands future, she offers realistic, practical guidance to anyone ready to put a lifetime of experience to work in a new age."

> Sally R. Luoma
> Director, Continuing Studies, Southern Methodist University

"Helen Harkness challenges her readers to banish the beliefs and mindless myths that block the creative use of the wisdom and experience of our current aging population."

> John Smale, M.D., Family Physician

DON'T STOP THE CAREER CLOCK

DON'T STOP THE CAREER CLOCK

Rejecting the Myths of Aging for a
New Way to Work in the 21st Century

Helen Harkness

Davies-Black Publishing
Palo Alto, California

Published by Davies-Black Publishing, an imprint of Consulting Psychologists Press, Inc., 3803 East Bayshore Road, Palo Alto, CA 94303; 800-624-1765.

Special discounts on bulk quantities of Davies-Black books are available to corporations, professional associations, and other organizations. For details, contact the Director of Book Sales at Davies-Black Publishing, an imprint of Consulting Psychologists Press, Inc., 3803 East Bayshore Road, Palo Alto, CA 94303; 650-691-9123; Fax 650-988-0673.

"The Ulyssean Sonnet" by John McLeish (pp. 187–188) is reproduced by kind permission of James R. Varey, literary executor for the late John A. B. McLeish.

03 02 01 00 99   10 9 8 7 6 5 4 3 2 1
Printed in the United States of America

Library of Congress Cataloging-in-Publication Data
Harkness, Helen
        Don't stop the career clock : rejecting the myths of aging for a new way
to work in the 21st century / Helen Harkness.
            p.   cm.
        Includes bibliographical references and index.
        ISBN 0-89106-127-4
        1. Career changes—United States. 2. Age and employment—United States.
        3. Aged—Employment—United States.
    I. Title.
    HF5384.H372   1999
    650.14′084′6—dc21   98-45341
                                                                              CIP

FIRST EDITION
First printing 1999

As we move into the twenty-first century, our model for integrating aging and working is destructive, depressing, derisive, and deplorable. A new pattern to effectively integrate our rapidly aging population into the workforce is essential, and yet for individuals and society to redesign, develop, and implement this will be perhaps the greatest challenge of the new millennium. It will require that we recognize, break, and discard countless, often unconscious, deeply held beliefs that are no longer valid. It will also require that we use our creative foresight and instincts to recognize and act on the changes in our work world. And finally, it will require us to design an action plan for a new way to age.

Our society collectively, and most of us individually, have a phobia about aging and the related work problems it creates. In my previous book, *The Career Chase* (1997), I focused on the fear of change and the emotional issues that surface as we recast and refocus our careers. *Don't Stop the Career Clock* sounds a clarion call for individuals and organizations to create an aging and working paradigm to match the rapidly changing realities of the current age, which is vastly different from any we have known. This is absolutely not our parents' work world or our grandparents' model of aging. It is imperative that we each take a leadership role in designing and implementing a new model for both aging and working, and in integrating it into our culture.

Central to this new reality is the fact that we will likely have an additional twenty to thirty or more healthy years to add to our life beyond traditional retirement age—a second midlife. My goal is to provide readers with the information, motivation, and tools they need to begin a new career during this potentially productive period. The fear related to changing careers will diminish as more people in our society successfully move through the transition and as we drop the outdated belief that "one life equals one career."

Knowing what we want and expect from our radically changing world can mean the difference between our success and failure. I would be delighted if I could say that determining this is a quick-fix process, but it is a complex and challenging one. Achieving this goal requires breaking through conscious and unconscious outdated belief barriers, negotiating a steep learning curve, carefully evaluating the realities of our digital age, and acquiring the personal and professional innovation and creativity necessary to thrive.

Despite our critical shortage of knowledge workers, ageism has held us back from capitalizing on the older population as an economic resource. We must discard the myths telling us that age equals biological, mental, psychological, and creative decline. Shaking loose from these beliefs, gaining insight into the changing workplace, and making the internal and external changes necessary to age successfully is what this book is all about. I have used my clients' stories, often in their own words, to illustrate the ability of older adults to succeed in our changing age—to be their own bosses and make their own decisions on how, when, and where to live and work.

My mantra for successful aging is "Live long and die fast." So this book is not about old age, which is ideally the last three to five years of life, regardless of chronological age. My message, which applies to people of all ages, is that we must stop designing and living our lives on the basis of chronological time, and focus instead on functional age.

This book is divided into three parts. Part One, "Rejecting the Myths of Aging and Working," confronts, with verifiable facts and research findings, the negative beliefs about aging that affect the older adult's participation in and contribution to society, and that consequently severely limits his or her self-actualization in what could be the most productive life period. Part Two, "Learning a New Way to Tell Time," introduces a focus on telling time functionally rather than chronologically. I present the Ulyssean model—in which the later years are viewed as a time of wisdom, creativity, power, and purpose—and an action plan for rethinking retirement and cultivating wisdom. Part Three, "Resetting the Career Clock," presents action steps and exercises for resetting the career clock and provides a discussion of free agents and entrepreneurs.

While I have accumulated applicable data and statistics from many reliable sources, I always use statistics rather uneasily, keeping in mind what Mark Twain is credited with saying: "We have liars, damned liars, and statistics." I am also aware that even the most objective researcher can find statistics to prove almost any point and fail to see information that does not fit his or her expectations. Admittedly, as a teacher and an advocate of a better way to age and work, I may be biased toward the optimistic. However, while these studies and statistics may not be as absolute as they indicate, they can at least be counted on to reveal major trends. The key point is that we, as interested and involved individuals, must begin to question for ourselves the validity of accepted rules of aging and working—and pave the way toward resetting the career clock.

Helen Leslie Harkness, Ph.D.
December 1998

Without my clients and their career issues, my ideas and perceptions would forever wander about in conceptual shadows. My concrete accomplishments in writing and in working on careers are tied directly to the reality facing my clients, from whom I learn daily. Their work-related problems are the touchstone and motivation for my ongoing search for more creative, effective ways to understand and to thrive in our rapidly changing world.

A special note of appreciation to Miss Bonnie, my mother-in-law, who at 95 validates all positive and successful aging characteristics—I value her as a role model in her aging journey. Decades ago Miss Bonnie urged me to write.

I am especially grateful to my large extended family: my grandparents, parents, and aunts, who provided an extremely healthy model for thriving throughout the entire life span; my fun-loving sister Madolyn, chronologically older than I but perhaps younger in spirit, who pushes and supports all my work; and my children and grandchildren, who inspire and move me always. I am also grateful to my very special group of personal friends who, through the years, have demonstrated wisdom in their lives for me to observe and value.

An extraordinary appreciation to Shelley Fleming—my translator, typist, reader, and editor. Without her talent and tolerance, my manuscript would not have made it. I highly value my publishers at Davies-Black, Melinda Adams Merino, Lee Langhammer Law, and Laura Simonds, for their energy, patience, and professionalism.

 **Helen Harkness,** Ph.D., founded Career Design Associates, Inc. (CDA), in the Dallas-Ft. Worth metroplex in 1978. CDA focuses on career life as the connecting point between individuals and organizations, thus linking career renewal with organizational change. A creative and resourceful strategist, catalyst, and teacher, Harkness is driven by her CDA credo, "Freedom Is Knowing Your Options." She is a pioneer in the research, development, and implementation of career management programs and resources to assist individuals with worklife transitions. Her goal is to loosen the confining chains of mindless myths that destroy contemporary careers, and to teach adults how to understand and thrive in their work in an age of change and chaos.

In 1976, based on her doctoral research, Harkness established in her local public library the first "one-stop" career job search center. Within one year, 3,000 adults had attended the center's workshops and an additional 3,000 had used its telephone information and referral services.

In 1989, Harkness's individual and organizational CDA clients founded the Pathfinders for the Future Think Tank, a group that meets monthly to explore, research, and forecast workplace trends. Harkness produced an educational documentary series of eight videotapes, *Careers in Finance* and *Discovering Career Options with the Self-Directed Search,* featuring Dr. John Holland. Each semester, she teaches several courses, including *Re-careering: The Search for Meaning, Money, Creativity, and Control* at Southern Methodist University in Dallas, and *Career Transitions for Lawyers* and *Career Options for Teachers.* As an organizational consultant, Harkness has designed and implemented career programs to identify and build employee skills to increase productivity and job satisfaction. Experienced and dynamic, she is much in demand as a speaker on career issues.

Harkness's work through Career Design Associates reflects and integrates her own multidimensional career as an entrepreneur in business and investment; a former academic dean/provost, college professor, and director of continuing education; and a director of human services in city government. She is author of numerous articles on career management and organizational effectiveness and of the book *The Career Chase: Taking Creative Control in a Chaotic Age* (1997).

Helen Harkness, Ph.D.
Career Design Associates, Inc.
2818 South Country Club Road
Garland, Texas 75043
tel: 972-278-4701 fax: 972-278-7092
options@career-design.com
www.career-design.com

Introduction

The most successful people are those who do all year long what they would otherwise do on their summer vacation.

—Mark Twain

We in the twenty-first century, in spite of living in a fast-moving and chaotic world, have an extraordinary advantage over previous generations: through improved nutrition, fitness, lifestyle changes, and medical research, we can anticipate an extra twenty to thirty years of healthy living. If these extra years are handled wisely, our middle age will double dramatically into a new second midlife, while our "old" age shrinks.

The fact that we have these extra years does not automatically grant happiness and a perfect life, for we must take an active hand in managing our windfall. The development of our second midlife requires us to creatively rethink our ideas of aging and working and to gain a new view of time itself.

Unfortunately, we have few positive aging role models or appropriate patterns to follow on how to capitalize on these additional healthy years, and those we do have are considered extremely unusual or are simply unnoticed. Most role models presented to us are not even marginally close to being a fit for our future aging!

The current model of aging and working dictates that we accumulate academic degrees (preferably with skills attached), find a lifetime mate, birth and rear our children, and achieve all major financial and career goals by the age of 40, or 45 at the latest. If we live to be 100, as countless of us will, what will we do with the last fifty years of our life?

Learning to use this extra time to create the best, most productive years of our life, however we define them, will require us to examine our conscious and unconscious fears about aging and take planned action steps now that will prevent us from stopping our career clock.

This will be a real challenge for people and organizations, since many of our attitudes, policies, and laws are still deeply rooted in nineteenth-century views of time, age, and work. Shaking ourselves loose from these will be difficult. While they may have served society's needs in the machine-oriented industrial age, they will not serve the needs of today's knowledge workers.

For a full life, aging and working are tied together. Whether teachers, executives, chefs, engineers, nurses, or florists, successful people seem to have one thing in common—they love what they do, and they stay on a learning curve. When work isn't allowing growth that's satisfying, we begin to feel and act old. Regardless of age, feelings of entrapment in our work life are a symbolic symptom of the dying, withering process. It is imperative that we understand the emerging realities and opportunities for aging and working.

The first step in successfully integrating aging and working is to know ourselves and our changing world and to understand that many of the rules under which we labor and the expectations that society expects us to fulfill are based on faulty ideas and incomplete data. For example, we should know that in the past, studies on aging have focused primarily on the 5 percent of the old who are sick or diseased. Consequently, we know very little about physically and mentally healthy aging adults.

Our lives are increasingly diverse and uncertain; there is no standard life cycle to follow, so we must make our own. Those at midlife, or even second midlife, today are the pathfinders for the future. We must now face the issues that keep us from evolving and leading continually useful, vital, productive lives throughout our entire life span, regardless of its length.

Fear of Aging

When a bright young woman caught in an ill-fitting career emphatically declares, "I can't change my career at this stage, I'm thirty-seven years old—I don't have time to start again!" or when an energetic man who has run a major company says that at fifty-five he is too old to begin a new enterprise, I know for certain that a new model for our aging and working that involves resetting our career clocks is a critical need. Just as there is a fear of a career change in my adult clients, which I discussed in *The Career Chase*, aging is a companion fear of equal or perhaps even greater weight that blocks our quest for meaningful work at midlife. For many talented adults, this intense fear and negative view of aging irrationally impedes career and life decisions and direction at a critical time of reevaluation.

This is not to say that all fears regarding aging and working are irrational. The fear of being cut from competition because of age rather than ability involves a real possibility, since we know that age discrimination is alive in the workplace and in our society. Misinformation about aging must be defused in our society and in the workplace as well as inside each individual. However, the focus of this book is to help individuals so they can get on with a creative approach to their work life without a great loss of time.

Our goal should be to redesign our aging model to integrate our age and work, making our current and later life a more friendly and familiar and a less stressful and frightening experience. I know from my in-depth career work with hundreds of adults, even those who are highly professional with much education and apparent success, that many adults don't begin to realize their potential or, as we say, "come into their own" until their life is half or even two-thirds over. My observations confirm Jung's belief that it takes one about fifty years simply to assemble and truly identify the real self.

It is absurd to begin to close ourselves down at a prime time of high potential for growth. It is mindless for us to drag along outdated conventional wisdom and myths on age and work and use them to guide our actions. The second half of life can be the best, but we must be determined to make it the best in spite of the current ageism in our culture, by overcoming our fears of aging. We must look at aging and working, at the current disorder and problems that come with these, and then create new realities by weaving together these two very critical areas of our life.

We must redirect our thinking and planning by using *functional age* instead of chronological age and by viewing work, however *we* define it, as a major source of positive energy in our life. This is true for anyone, regardless of age, who fears or dreads aging, but especially for those who are in midlife, or perhaps past it, and who search for a meaningful direction for the last half of their life. My goal is to help clear through the clutter of misinformation, myth, misguided belief, and "conventional wisdom" about aging and work to help free those paralyzed by uncertainty, fear of the unknown, lack of information on options, and the chaos of our changing times.

Our intuitive wisdom and honed instincts, using what I have labeled our *third eye* and *third ear*, need to be at center stage now. A basic premise of this book is that what seemed true and certain in the past, or even in the present, may now have become a mindless myth, regardless of its revered position. We cannot move through our changing world loaded with outdated, thoughtless beliefs and generally accepted "truths" that direct us off course. We need a healthy, positive, questioning skepticism and not a cynical, turned-off, negative, or suspicious approach to our world. This requires information, careful listening, and asking questions that are meaningful to us. It is critical today to watch for the clichéd wisdom of conventional authority. If there ever were a time to think directly and clearly for oneself, to tune in, to listen, sharpen, and value our instincts and intuition, it is now.

Based on the belief that knowledge is power, an important goal is to bring together essential information that can help adults be better prepared to deal effectively and meaningfully with the inescapable: we are heading rapidly into a new way to age and work. The better we understand and integrate this, the better we can maintain creative control and direction of our life and career. If we ignore these rapidly accelerating forces, we will find ourselves alone and vulnerable.

The Grail Quest for Contemporary Adults

"What do I really want to do for my career?"

"I want to do something with meaning and purpose but I don't know what it is."

"I know what I don't want but I have no idea what I really want or would enjoy doing."

"I know what I would like to do but have no idea how to get there."

"At fifty, I've accomplished more than my wildest dreams—so what's next for me?"

"For the last half of my life I want to bridge the gulf between what I do and what I value."

I hear variations of these remarks daily from adults of all ages and occupations, and from all economic, social, academic, and professional levels. This is not aimless whining, but genuine questioning and searching from thoughtful and high-achieving adults.

Tying our work to meeting a deeper meaning is a natural evolution for adults today. For the generation following the Depression and World War II, the *job*—stable lifetime work that pays the bills—was the goal. Later, the achievers focused on a *career* in a particular profession such as law, banking, medicine, teaching, or management as the means to success. Today we are adding another dimension: discovering our *calling* or *vocation*—work with a deeper purpose or meaning, assuring us that each has something unique to offer.

All three—job, career, and calling—are related, but on very different levels. *Calling* is the higher overriding purpose that we feel from our heart—it feeds and revives our soul and spirit. Our particular job provides the fuel, the means to run or develop our career. *Career,* from the root word *carry* or *cart,* can be seen as the means we use to move to our calling. Filling a need, making a life, not just making a living, is essential for a full life.

Feeling that we are born with a reason for being, a purpose, and that we must discover and act on it is in direct contrast to our culture's adherence to the Lockean assumption that human beings are most deeply motivated by economic concerns. Ferguson (1993) contends that beyond a certain level of material sufficiency, other strong needs are clearly taking precedence: the desire to be healthy, to be loved, to feel competent, to participate fully in a community, and to have meaningful employment. For millions, new attitudes toward work, career choice, and consumption are slowly replacing materialism and creating a social and business ethic more characterized by concern for the quality of life, appropriate technology, entrepreneurship, decentralization, ecology, and spirituality.

To discover what is deeply important to us—our calling—we must first stop and listen to our own inner voice to determine what we really want, as opposed to what we have been talked into. If work is rewarding, not just obligatory, it reorders our values and priorities. Today our new paradigm of values is slowly moving center stage to replace the former paradigm of economics, with its emphasis on growth, control, manipulation, and the race to see who dies with the most money. Leider (1998) sums up the new model simply: "The good life means living in the place where you belong, being with people you love, doing the right work—on purpose" (p. 14).

Work without purpose or meaning is deadly. Dossey (1995) points out that job dissatisfaction and the joyless striving that accompanies it are greater causes of heart attack than high cholesterol or fatty diets, and that more heart attacks occur between 8:00 A.M. and 9:00 A.M. on Monday mornings than at any other time.

Without the opportunity for expressing creativity, people are unlikely to ever find happiness in their work, according to Fox (1994). He urges us to overcome our feelings of isolation, insecurity, and alienation in our work life and to see a world where the self is not sacrificed for a job, but where intellect, heart, and health come together in a harmony of essential life experiences that celebrates the whole person. Good living and good working go together, and we are now redefining the role and rewards of work in our life.

Many of my clients originally bought into the idea of conventional success and status and now, despite the financial trappings of success, are feeling a deep poverty of the heart and soul. Their search for meaning and calling is not a quick transition that is simple and painless. Their Grail Quest involves a process of integrating internal self-discovery and the external shifting and changing environmental realities.

My own experience and years of keen observation, research, and direct interaction with my clients have shown me that the middle and later years of our life can be the best, if filled with a meaningful purpose, new growth, learning, creativity, and a measure of control over our destiny. I stress this not only as a helpful, hopeful, inspirational, motivational message, but also as a provable, research-based, observable reality. Men and women in their later years can, if they choose, develop and maintain their powers to produce, learn, and create until the very end of life's journey. However, to accomplish this requires that we break through our negative belief barriers that render us prematurely old.

To break through these conventional belief barriers, we must first look at the rapidly shifting external landscape and the current realities of our changing culture and work world. It is essential that we explore the new research on aging, along with fluctuating workplace trends and forces so that we may capitalize on and integrate new possibilities into our career/life plan. At the same time, we must recognize and actively reject the cultivation of ageism in our culture along with our own personal fears about aging.

There are countless aging myths based on misinformation and mindlessness that are directly contrary to current reliable research. If we fail to reexamine this research and factor it into our future, we remain frozen in our past expectations of aging. For us to cut off our livelihood and welfare because of these past beliefs—these unexamined but generally accepted guidelines—is expensive, wasteful, and bordering on tragic for millions of individuals and for our society itself.

Most of us will be living at least an extra twenty, thirty, or even forty healthy years, and the next generations could live much longer. The real problem is that we have few healthy aging role models to follow, and with these, "reshaping our personal futures will be difficult and the penalty for being unprepared will be long years of poverty and stagnation" (Cetron and Davies, 1998).

We are on a new frontier of how to live and work creatively and successfully until the last day we live. We must be the pathfinders, leading the way on how to make significant changes in our work life at midlife and beyond. We can do this by concentrating on functional age—ignoring chronology and learning a new way to tell time, re-careering and rethinking retirement, moving from career crisis to career quest, creating and activating what I call a *capstone career*. By knowing what we want and doing what we love, we can continue life's journey with creativity, wisdom, power, and purpose.

A Personal Odyssey

As a career change teacher I remember Mark Twain's admonition "You can't no more teach what you don't know, than come back from where you ain't been." When it comes to integrating aging and working in our contemporary culture, I've been there, very actively, for many years. My interest in a new way to integrate age and work is an extension of my own experience as well as that of my older adult college students in the 1970s, and is validated by my thirty years of research and experience working directly with thousands of adults in the career change and enhancement process. My basic interest in a new way to age and work started during my doctoral training, when we were taught that our mental and sexual powers peaked between the ages of seventeen and twenty-one—and from then on it was all downhill.

This nonsense activated my common sense factor because, from the bevy of older adults in my own environment who were well into their eighties and nineties and were mentally sharp, active, and in charge of their life, I knew that this was ridiculous, flawed research. I knew that I had only just started using my own brain creatively, and I was twice seventeen at that time. Intuitively I knew that useful brain power did not decline after early adulthood, regardless of the current research (or lack of it) in the field of aging in the early 1970s.

My direct connection with the reality of aging stereotyping came in the mid-1970s. Near the time my male contemporaries were thinking of early retirement, I was elated to be starting my own company. I had spent the two previous decades as a 1950s model wife, working to send a husband through medical school. I then experienced the failure of my marriage, the tragic deaths of several close family members, a fire and home rebuilding, and rearing three teenagers as a single parent in the crazy world of the 1970s—where I didn't have a clue about the rules and realities—while working full-time as a college teacher and administrator. I completed a doctoral degree after an eight-year part-time schedule, not in English as originally planned, but in higher education, focusing directly on the subject of career change, which I knew would be a major need for society in the near future.

I was excited and finally ready, experiencing fully what Barbara Hubbard and a roomful of female participants at the 1995 meeting of the International World Future Society enthusiastically labeled "female vocational arousal"—the point in time that Jung (1933) describes for women at midlife who have followed the traditional wife/mother role and who then decide to use the "sharpness of mind" and take on the challenges of the more competitive outside work world.

All of my juggling—while constantly keeping straight which were my "glass balls" (my children, my students, and my learning curve, not to be dropped at any cost) and which were the less important but numerous "rubber balls" (which could be dropped and perhaps picked up later)—had finally paid off. I had traveled throughout the country, researching adults and their careers in major libraries and questioning psychologists, academics, research professors, and employment agencies. At last I was creating my own career consulting firm integrating my doctoral research with my own experience, education, and mission. I was very aware that I was a bit ahead of my time in setting up a full-time business to teach adults how to manage their careers more effectively, but I saw it as an important emerging societal need.

Incidentally, a marketing consultant strongly advised that I could not have a successful business operating out of my house—professionals would expect a more high-rise image and glitz. Since I had six thousand square feet and a ten-acre yard to maintain anyway, it made sense to use it, which has worked extremely well for me for twenty years. I resolved to consciously maintain high competence, commitment, and creativity to impress clients, rather than an address. Paradoxically, as our times have changed, my office arrangement has become the envy of many. Again I remind myself and others to use their instincts and common sense, and beware the tyranny of professional authorities. If what is advised doesn't instinctively ring true for you, put it aside and move confidently, realizing you may indeed only be ahead of your time!

Since incorporation of the business was the next step, I made an appointment with my attorney, telling him only that I was making a major change in my work life, but giving no specific details. He immediately opened our meeting by outlining options for stashing my assets into a bank trust for protection and management during my immediate and, as he assumed, pending retirement years. After all, I was the same age as his mother! Stunned at what I was hearing, I mumbled my thanks and fled!

Since that time, I have enjoyed my capstone career. Daily I learn, grow, understand, create, teach, and control my life—

sometimes brilliantly and frequently less so, but on my own terms—and I remain on a learning curve always. Rather than avoiding and fearing change, ambiguity, and complexity, I seek and thrive on them. Having experienced repeated setbacks, failures, and disappointments, and having moved through and beyond them to what I perceive to be a higher level, I now know that whatever happens, I will somehow land on my feet and thrive.

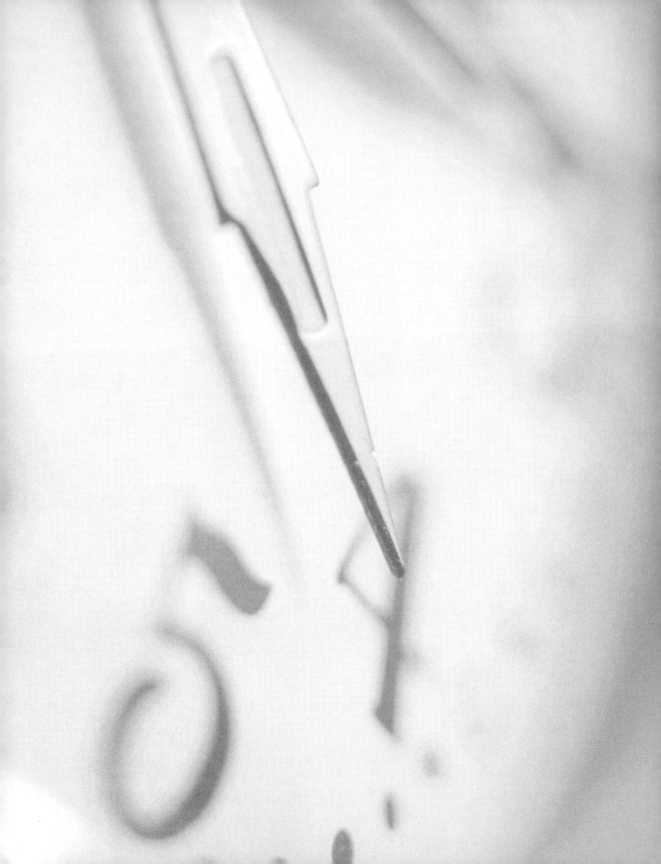

PART ONE

Rejecting the Myths of Aging and Working

Myths, the stories that guide our lives, are so deeply ingrained that we seldom consciously think of them. They are archetypal, unconsciously inherited from our ancestors, our culture, and our society. Unfiltered, unproved, and unexamined, these collective beliefs are accepted uncritically and many times can be used to justify unsound attitudes and practices. We process what we see through myths. Our perception then becomes "reality," and additional beliefs continue to be made to correspond to this reality. Voltaire said that those who believe in absurdities will commit atrocities, and many of our accepted behaviors and beliefs about aging today are absurdities indeed.

Part One focuses on beliefs, myths, stereotypes, and misinformation about aging, in society and in the workplace, that negatively affect the way we age and work. Debunking these myths will be no simple matter. It presents a challenge for our society—for the majority of the aging themselves, who have obligingly accepted these beliefs, as well as for the younger people who are keenly aware of the negative aspects of aging. It involves breaking through the brick wall of denial and directly facing the issues of aging that are critical for living and working in the twenty-first century.

Biogerontology, the biology of aging, is only about forty years old, and therefore facts are scarce and conclusions often more speculative than those in better-established scientific disciplines. Leonard Hayflick is one of its most respected pioneers. Hayflick (1994) lists three reasons for the lack of serious research into aging: (a) some scientists believe that prolonging life is not scientifically possible, or morally or economically desirable; (b) others are ageist and consider this science dull—that is, age is intractable, an absolute certainty, and the old live too long anyway; and (c) the aging process itself is highly complex, with many causes and mechanisms operating simultaneously.

In former times, questions about aging, mortality, and immortality were largely the province of philosophy and religion, since old age and death were accepted as inevitable consequences of life. But there has been a recent surge of interest in what scientists have learned about aging and how this knowledge can be applied to controlling or even reversing the aging process.

Before this century, only one out of ten lived to age sixty-five; today it is 80 percent. We unfortunately know little about *healthy* aging. Common sense says we grow old because we wear out, but actually no wear-and-tear theory of aging exists. So we really have few certainties, and many of the ideas about aging we have accepted as absolutes are merely myths, not true in fact. Our beliefs about aging need to be examined and altered to fit newer circumstances and information.

CHAPTER ONE

Aging as Physical and Psychological Decline

Shattering the Myth That Growing Up
Means Running Down

Youth, large, lusty, loving—youth, full of grace, force, fascination.
Do you know that old age may come after you with equal grace,
force, fascination?

—Walt Whitman, *Youth, Old Age, and Night*

There is no way we can look forward to our aging if we see the journey that is life as moving upward to a peak in our forties and then abruptly dropping off into a period of physical decline in which we remain suspended for forty or fifty years until our eventual death. The reality can be far different—age does not automatically spell decline. Aging is not all about being frail, dependent, and nonproductive. It can be a time of freedom, options, and choices, more than we have ever experienced. Vital men and women do not tell you that they would want to relive their earlier years. In one study of older adults, Schaie (1994) had some surprising findings:

- Adolescence and the thirties were the least satisfying years; and 20 percent said the teenage years were their least satisfying years.

- 19 percent identified their fifties as their most satisfying years.

- 18 percent named their sixties and seventies as the most satisfying years, while only 6 percent named their sixties and seventies as their least satisfying years.

- 8 percent said their eighties were their most satisfying years.

Our fear of old age and death, reinforced by the ageism in our society, can cause us to slow down and develop an inferiority complex at the age of maturity, a time that could provide our best, most productive, and most thoughtful years. This fear creates in us the habit of thinking about dying instead of making the most of the life we have.

I believe that much of this focusing on death and aging is due to an absence of purpose or direction, or the lack of suitable or valued occupation. In other words, the minds of many are filled only with the fear of being old. This fear is more prevalent among the aged, but often those more youthful can also be victims. The greatest of all remedies for the fear of age and death is a *burning desire for achievement, backed by useful service to others.* Busy people seldom have time to worry about dying. They find life too exciting to fold up their tent and steal away.

What happens to us in our work life and how we adjust to it strongly affect our feelings on aging and dying. We may begin our career with great expectations and zest. Yet somewhere along the way—sometimes because our expectations were unreal to start with, or because of external barriers, or both—we realize we aren't going to achieve all the lofty goals or the perfect state we had planned. In the 1960s I recall reading an article that said if an ambitious woman had a Ph.D. and talent, she could be president of a university—a worthy goal, I thought. However, when I completed the Ph.D. in the 1970s, after rearing three children, the "gypsy scholar" was in, and nontenured part-time college teaching jobs were the norm. Instead of giving up, I became president of my own company—which turned out to be a great decision. Frequently the path to success, intended to bring us all things perfect, is really an obstacle course, and we may discover that our greatest obstacle is the inability to discover alternative options to keep us progressing.

Lack of growth, the feeling of being stagnant, increases our sensitivity to aging and to our own mortality. If we remain in this state of mind, frozen and paralyzed, we can develop a malaise—vague feelings of illness and depression, uncertainty, unfocused unhappiness, and alienation. We may feel we are losing control over events and begin to question our goals, to suspect unfair treatment, or to see ourselves as failures, trapped and pessimistic about our future.

If we remain poorly adjusted, but still on the job, we often retire without resigning, though with the current downsizing fever this may not be an option. We may develop the Sisyphus Syndrome (Harkness, 1997), mindlessly pushing a heavy boulder up a steep mountain each day for all eternity, only to have it roll back down again. We may reminisce about the "good old days," avoid real responsibility, communicate poorly with others, refuse promotions, live for time outside of work, daydream, and focus on mindless tasks. We may drink, smoke, waste time, complain about being bored, and find fault with all. This disillusionment on the job can also result in poor personal adjustment.

If privately we see ourselves as a failure, we may talk of success but unconsciously seek defeat. Some at midlife may fantasize, sprint off, and leave their families in search of the "fountain of youth." Others live "life's lie" and deny their lack of satisfaction, freeze over, and wait for something they cannot name. And some spend the second half of life wandering in search of an unknown or unattainable goal.

Those who adjust well do take control of their work life, redefine their goals, and modify career-related aspects of their dreams. These adults engage in genuine self-renewal and growth. They develop flexibility and an identity that carries them across their life span. They avoid engaging in self-destructive behavior and burning up energy in anxiety. They manage tension well and fully understand that self-pity and resentment, on or off the job, are toxic.

Physical Decline

It is critical that we examine the current reality of aging— biological as well as mental, psychological, and social—and change the totally negative picture imprinted by our earlier perceptions. Research is finding that much of what we thought was physical decline due to fundamental physical aging is really disease.

Our beliefs and myths grow out of social conditions that set up aging expectations. The fear around the deep belief that we are meant to grow old, feeble, and senile can actually create a false aging—a self-fulfilling prophecy generated by a withering self-image. Chopra (1993) goes so far as to say that aging as decline has a hidden connection that it is so strong our bodies actually conform to it. A sense of decline, loss, feebleness in mind and body, helplessness, and loss of control has character- ized much of our concept of aging. We need to overturn our fear- based beliefs.

Strong social support—including all the things that bind people together, such as language, customs, family structure, and social tradition—is known to be an important factor in physical health. For example, people with a strong social support system live longer after heart attack, and men with prostate cancer live three years longer on average if married ("We Are Not Lone Wolves," 1998).

Much of what we thought was an inevitable part of the aging process is social conditioning. We can adopt new beliefs and unlearn the behavior that's making us age. Seeing aging as physical decline, as a disease no one wants to admit he or she has since the aged are mainly sickly, bedridden, and stashed in nursing homes, is a deadly stereotype.

The reality is that society, the media, and physicians—even gerontologists—have focused on the 6 to 15 percent of elders who are frail and ill. But the majority of older people are in good physical shape. Older people actually get fewer acute illnesses than young people, and only 16 percent rate their health as poor.

Chronic disability among people over sixty-five began to decline in 1992, and this decline has since accelerated, according to the National Long-Term Care Surveys. Currently, about 21 percent of people over sixty-five have a chronic disability that impairs daily activity to some degree, compared with roughly 25 percent in 1982. A number of long-term trends may account for the decline in disability, including improvements in medical therapy (such as antihypertensive medication) and lifestyle factors (notably a decrease in smoking rates; "30% Pick Death Over Nursing Homes," 1997).

Each person is born a unique individual, and the interaction of aging and life experience increases the variability of physical as well as mental and psychological performances across the life span. Motor performance of the elderly is highly variable. Today we see some eighty-year-olds who require daily care in nursing centers and others who are living independently and even running marathons. Physiological changes occur with age and these may limit motor performance, but no "average" behavior can be specified. It is difficult to tell if specific physiological changes are due entirely to aging or to declining motivation, lower societal expectations, or occurrence of disease (Spirduso and MacRae, 1990).

Researcher Waneen Spirduso, a motor learning expert at the University of Texas at Austin, strongly maintains that it is never too late to take up a new sport. In spite of the theory that the functions of the central nervous system, such as reaction time, slow after age twenty-five, that doesn't mean our ability to learn a physical activity suffers. "When it comes to mastering simple motor-skills tasks, older people are just as coordinated as younger people—even if they can't perform the tasks as quickly," says Spirduso (1997). One of her experiments involved several dozen subjects—half who were age sixty or older, the other half around twenty—performing tasks such as moving their hands from one place to another in response to certain stimuli. In each test, the older individuals learned as quickly as the younger ones.

The National Center for Health Statistics surveyed the ability of 38.3 million individuals to perform work-related activities (Kovar and LaCroix, 1987). The population sample included individuals from fifty-five to seventy-four years old who had worked at some time after they were forty-five. The results showed that overall, 58 percent of this population had no difficulty with any of the work-related activities. Potentially, many who retired for reasons other than their health could have stayed on the job. The activities that depended on lower body strength caused the greatest problems for those who were older. They had more problems with mobility, endurance, and general lower body strength, whereas those activities related to freedom of movement and fine motor skills were much less affected by age. Substantial data exist to support the hypothesis that a lifestyle of systematic physical activity may maintain a person's physical capacity and thereby delay the age at which environmental demands exceed physical capabilities (Charness and Bosman, 1990). In the 1960s exercise was thought to be dangerous for people over fifty. Today we know that meeting nutritional requirements and exercise are the most important factors in staying healthy when we are older.

In one study, Timothy Salthouse (cited in White, 1993) compared a group of very fast and accurate typists of college age with another group in their sixties. Both groups typed sixty words per minute. The older typists, it turned out, achieved their speed by making fewer finger movements, which saved a fraction of a second here and there, and by reading ahead in the text. The neural networks involved in typing appear to have been reshaped to compensate for losses in motor skills or other age changes.

A 1994 study at Tufts University (cited in Restak, 1997) showed it's never too late for building muscle. Frail elders in nursing homes showed improvement (a 10 percent addition of muscle mass) as a result of exercise, leading to improvements in strength of more than 100 percent over a ten-week period.

According to a report in the *Harvard Health Newsletter* ("Keep Walking; Keep Living," 1998), older adults who walked the equivalent of thirty minutes six times per month had a 43 percent lower death rate than those who were sedentary. However, nearly three in ten adults sixty-five and older report no leisure time physical activity according to the American Medical Association.

To better understand aging in the knowledge workers of today, it might be worthwhile to compare them to academics rather than to the blue-collar worker who uses a physical set of skills. "We should alter our concept of what *very old age* is when we discuss academics," says Birren (1990). Academics age better because they have a healthy lifestyle, useful information, and less exposure to noxious conditions of the environment, which is also true of information and knowledge workers today. Birren contends, and I strongly agree, that many of these people are capable of high productivity to eighty years of age and beyond.

Sexual Decline

Many years ago, my marvelously romantic eighty-two-year-old aunt lived with me for a decade after outliving two husbands. Before she married for the third time, I asked her how an eighty-two-year-old felt about sex. Her reply: "Well, I feel about the same way I did when I was twenty."

According to Dr. Ruth B. Weg (cited in Kanin, 1978), the expression of our sexuality very much relates to other parts of our being. Often sexual interest and activity in old age are considered unacceptable and discouraged, in spite of overwhelming evidence that sexual desire and capacity continue well into the later years. Many elders have bought into this myth, hesitating to admit to having sexual desires or feeling guilty, ashamed, or embarrassed about them.

However, some studies have shown a positive correlation between sexual activity and longer life. For example, a study of 1,000 men aged forty-five to fifty-nine reported in the *British Medical Journal* found that men who have frequent sex are less likely to die at an early age. A decade later, they found the death rate from all causes for the men who were the least sexually active was twice as high as that of the most sexually active group ("Sex May Prolong Life," 1998).

Our sexuality is tied closely to our self-image, part of which is tied into our identity as a worker. Older men in particular may not be able to function as well sexually when forced to retire. They may feel "less a man," and tie that into an expression that is sexual. For many, however, sex can continue, and even improve, with age.

Bortz (1991) reports on a 1984 study by Edward Brecher titled "Love, Sex and Aging." Among the 4,246 participants, who ranged in age from fifty to ninety-three, the study found that the following percentages of people were sexually active:

- 93 percent of women and 98 percent of men in their fifties

- 81 percent of women and 91 percent of men in their sixties

- 65 percent of women and 79 percent of men in their seventies

Health is definitely not an overriding factor associated with productivity in advanced age until late in life. From a longitudinal research study on men and women over the age of seventy carried out in Golhenborg, Sweden, it would appear that physical changes associated with advancing age do not become a predominant limiting feature of life for most adults until eighty-five years of age, and may occur even later for academics. In a study of scientific publications of people in varying age groups, no one age was found to be the most productive, thus supporting the conclusion that age cannot be used as a surrogate criterion for creativity (Birren, 1990).

A key point we must realize is that individuals adjust their activities in accord with expectations of their institutional surroundings. Birren states that "the removal of a fixed retirement age in academic institutions would undoubtedly have a large effect on productivity. . . . It would appear that our expectations for a healthy long life are underestimated and, in a similar way, our expectations for creativity and productivity with age are underestimated."

The Mind-Body Connection

Western medicine is just beginning to use the mind-body connection—the biological and the psychological components that together create the power of intention. The work of Nuland (1994, 1998), a medical doctor whose interest in living and dying is as much philosophical as medical, maintains that the body is much greater than the sum of its parts. The critical factor, he says, is the will to live, the internal wisdom coming from the soul. Until now, Western thought has maintained that the body is a mindless machine. We do know that the incidence of cancer is lower in people who have a strong sense of purpose and well-being, and that cancer patients who are given psychological therapy survive twice as long as those who are not (Chopra, 1993). Chopra notes that a placebo reduces pain in 30 percent of the cases in which it is used. A placebo is an inert substance; the power that activates it is the power of suggestion alone. The body is capable of producing a biochemical response once the mind has been given the appropriate suggestion. This suggestion is converted into the body's intention to cure itself.

If we feel old, regardless of our chronological age, we will be unhappy. If we feel young, we will adjust to aging better. Our fear of aging and our deep-seated belief that we are meant to grow old at a certain chronological age frequently become a self-fulfilling prophecy (Comfort, 1976).

The Psychology of Aging

The psychology of aging is concerned with patterns of changes in individuals as they mature and grow old. The field is now in a phase of rapid expansion, but it was slow to develop, with early psychologists studying behavior patterned after successes in the hard sciences of chemistry and physics. Consequently, just like the literature in physiological aging, the psychology of aging became a litany of decline in the mental adaptive capacities of humans. Birren and Schaie (1996) contend that the psychology of aging is now poised for a metamorphosis into a more complex and sophisticated subject matter and perhaps a more useful one. . . . Pressure for knowledge about processes of aging arises not only because of the practical needs of an aging society but also because science is coming to realize that there is a need for deeper insights into the principles of the dynamics of development of aging. (p. 17)

There may be more differences than similarities in the psychological aging process. Gerodynamics, based on general systems theory, particularly the second law of thermodynamics and the modern chaos theory, is a recent term for a comprehensive inclusive theory of aging that integrates the biological, behavioral, and social processes of aging.

According to Birren and Schaie (1996), the aging of living systems can be defined as the self-organizing process of increasing entropy with age, which creates more disorder than order and results in the system's death. Self-organization in this case is a process by which a structure or pattern of change emerges with time. In short, increasing disorderly and orderly structures increases uniqueness. Gerodynamics is the basis for a new theory, the branching theory of aging, which hypothesizes that there are typical patterns of stability and change in the form of a branching tree at the biological, behavioral, and social levels of the aging systems. Birren and Schaie believe that the concept of gerodynamics is sorely needed at this point to replace chronological age as the sole criterion for analyzing changes in the adult organism.

How Society Contributes to Physical and Psychological Aging

Comfort (1976) believes there are two kinds of aging. One type is biological: gray hair, loss of hearing, perhaps a lack of recuperative power from illness. While this loss of vigor is not yet fully understood, it is being looked at, especially in the field of experimental gerontology. Biological aging can be slowed down, though there is no agreement on how much. However, says Comfort, what makes oldness insupportable in human societies does not come from a consequence of this biological aging process, but arises from *sociogenic aging*—the role society imposes on people as they reach a certain chronological age. The retired are frequently rendered useless and impoverished. "After that transition, and in proportion to their chronological age, they are prescribed to be unintelligent, unemployable, crazy, and asexual" (p. 10).

"Successful aging" in our society is often characterized by decreased social interaction and emotional withdrawal from other people. Comfort (1976) says:

> Disengagement in our culture is often, alas, sludge language for being ejected, excluded or demeaned, and liking it—an attribute wished on the newly created old to plaster our guilt and provide a piece of jargon to excuse our conduct. Age-proof people will have none of it. (p. 65)

The *disengagement theory* argues that aging people accept and even welcome withdrawal from society—the reduced interaction, activity, and commitment. Levin and Levin (1981) report that a dozen research studies discredit the disengagement theory by showing that life satisfaction increases with older people when they are active. But the theory continues to provide a "shabby rationalization for the poor treatment of old people in our youth- and task-oriented society and for the fear and hatred of old people as found even among gerontologists and geriatricians themselves" (p. 85).

Ageism is subtly blatant in our society, laws, and government programs. We need to examine how the gerontology researchers themselves have approached the study of the aging individual. What questions have they been asking about aging? What assumptions have they made? What findings have contributed to our view of aging? We realize that scientists frequently find what they expect to find, and may well disregard the unexpected.

Depression and Aging

George Vaillant, a Harvard psychologist, in his 1977 follow-up on the Grant Study of 185 students at Harvard started during World War II, found that being depressed often leads to premature aging, chronic illness, and early death. Depression is emotional numbness. A depressed person feels no laughter or joy inside because these positive emotions have been blocked by unhappy memories. Old unresolved traumas lurk inside, and when new positive feelings try to emerge, they are filtered through preexisting layers of hopelessness. Vaillant concluded that it was the long, continuing accumulation of lingering, unresolved, unfinished issues, not specific dramatic incidents, that created poor mental health. Of the 53 Grant Study participants who had the best mental health, only 2 died by the age of 53. Of the 48 with the poorest mental health, 18 were chronically ill or dead by that age.

Good mental health is a major factor in healthy aging. According to some professionals, a secure sense of self is generally formed early in life. However, from my work with adults at midlife, I know that a strong sense of personal power can be gained much later. Actually, when most of us get to our second midlife, we can be ready to take charge. It isn't stress that makes us sick, but rather giving up the inner adaptability to stress. The greatest threat to life and health in our midlife is having nothing to live for that matters to us.

The powerful risk effect of depression on health was stressed in a recent Johns Hopkins University study ("Depression in Later

Years," 1997). It was found that for anyone who has had a major depression, the risk of a heart attack soars to 4.5 times the normal. Even with the less severe dysthymia (sadness that is not as disabling as full-blown depression), the risk is twice as high as normal. Heart disease, America's number one killer, is certainly powerful evidence that mind and body are interconnected. Depression even increases the likelihood of stroke to three times the average.

Just as depression can lead to physical decline, the converse is also true. Researchers in the *American Journal of Psychiatry,* cited in "Health News" (1997), report that they found that *healthy* older adults are at no greater risk for depression than younger people. This is reassuring news for older adults in good health, but the study also showed that those with chronic illness and disability are particularly vulnerable to depression. A second study in the same journal found that older people who were depressed were more likely to die prematurely, from disease as well as from suicide. Other research has proven that depression slows recovery from illness, increases health care costs, and certainly affects the ability to live independently.

The recognition that depression, at all ages, can be treated and cured by chemical agents is a major breakthrough. Restak (1997) believes that depression can be the result of age-related alterations in the number of neurotransmitters, which can render the older brain somewhat more susceptible. In other words, according to Restak, older people could have more of a biological tendency to be depressed, but not so much if they keep physically healthy.

Often older people are reluctant to seek help for depression—because they do not want to admit their problem, they feel they are too old to be helped, or they hope the problem will go away on its own. But with new and effective medications available, treatment is highly successful (Stern, 1997).

Recognition of depression in the elderly is a matter of life and death, because older people in the United States have a higher rate of suicide than any other group. Studies show that 90 percent of the older Americans who commit suicide are clinically depressed, a condition that could have been helped or eliminated by medication (Stern, 1997).

The loss of a spouse, friends, and regular social exercise activities also increases the likelihood of depression in the elderly. Males seem to adjust less well to change—suicides are 35.5 per 100,000 for men aged sixty-five to seventy-four, and for those over eighty-five years, the rate rises to 61.6 per 100,000. "People are deteriorating and dying more out of anguish, depression, and lack of meaning than from bugs and germs," says Dychtwald (1979, p. 1). He emphasizes the idea that there are alternatives to viewing aging as a time of disease and despair only.

The real problem stems from lack of involvement and direction. Without this, when older employees feel a loss of personal control, they may become defensive and domineering at work. The sense of aging and the techniques used to avoid facing ourselves are directly tied to commitment and satisfaction. As I say repeatedly, retire *to* something, not just *from* something.

An important finding is that older persons are less likely to receive mental health care than younger people. Primary care physicians, like their emergency department counterparts, are unlikely to identify and treat psychiatric and psychological problems in older adults, or to refer them to mental health professionals, in part because the patients don't tell doctors they're depressed, because they don't know what it is, and they tend to be ashamed of these new feelings, says Barry D. Lebowitz, chief of research on aging at the National Institute of Mental Health (cited in Stern, 1997).

Elders are also less likely to receive mental health services than younger persons because it is somehow seen as useless to help them. Freud, who may have set the stage for later physicians, believed treating depression in patients over fifty was futile. In one of his earlier papers, "On Psychotherapy" (1959), he said: "Near and above the 50s the elasticity of the mental processes on which the treatment depends is, as a rule, lacking. Old people are no longer educable, and, on the other hand, the mass of material to be dealt with would prolong the treatment indefinitely." This negative attitude in the medical community on emotional as well as physical factors in aging amounts to ageism in its worst form, and unfortunately has not disappeared.

Generalizations about the responsiveness of elders to interventions are misleading or inaccurate. Today's older population is highly varied in demographic characteristics, past personal history, current health status, and psychological functioning. Currently, very systematic studies of the efficacy of psychoanalytic or psychodynamic treatment of older patients have positive results, showing significant improvement at the end of six months.

In summary, evidence clearly indicates that as people get older in our society, they have a strong tendency to be less happy, to hold more negative concepts about themselves, and experience a loss of confidence (Bischof, 1969). However, a great deal is left unexplained in the process affecting the adjustment of older people. The more an individual fears aging, the more negative his or her adjustment to old age will be. Scott is an example of a client who overcame his depression and began his most important growth at midlife.

Maintaining Control, Independence, and Self-Efficacy: Key to Physical and Psychological Health for the Aging

In the past, when Dr. Stephen Zarit, assistant director of Pennsylvania State University's Gerontology Center, was asked, "How

MYTH BUSTER : SCOTT'S STRATEGY

I first started thinking about changing careers almost a decade before I did. I remember where it first hit me. I was at a James Taylor concert. I had just received a big promotion and, by my own reasoning, should have felt great. Instead I was miserable. It was a boring corporate job that I had little interest in doing.

For the next eight to ten years, I swung back and forth, sometimes liking what I did, sometimes hating it. I changed jobs three times in that period, always taking another editing job, always thinking the job was the problem. It was—up to a point. But looking back, I realize that the industry was changing at the same time that my interests were changing. Also, my career path had taken me out of the work I really enjoyed—writing and creating—and into an area I despised: middle management. I came to believe that I was a failure, that I wasn't good at what I did. That ultimately, I believe, became a self-fulfilling belief.

Finally, totally depressed, I went to see a psychologist. After a couple of sessions, she advised me to seek career counseling. It was enlightening to say the least. Not only did I begin to focus on the real issues, but I also discovered that I wasn't alone. A lot of very successful people felt exactly as I did.

Within a year, I left my position at the paper after strategically negotiating a severance package (the paper folded only a few months later), and with three partners started my own media/editorial consulting practice. Although it grew very slowly, it was a wonderful experience. I didn't make much money, but I gained a wealth of self-confidence that I had completely lost, and—very important—I put my personal and professional life in much clearer perspective. My reliance on job security has been replaced by a self-reliance that can never be taken from me—an extremely important shift in this time of change. Finally, my faith in God grew tremendously.

After a year, while letting my partners continue to build the business, I took a position with a large international management consulting firm, making almost the same amount I was making when I left the newspaper. [This had increased considerably four years later.]

While I'm excited about my new position—it's the writing, editing, consulting, and creativity that I missed in my last career [Scott has since written two books for his organization]—I view it as much less paternalistic than I did my past career. I could well retire here. At the same time, I could use this as a vehicle to successfully navigate whatever the continuum of change throws my way. Either way, I'll be happy.

Am I glad I changed careers? You bet.

can I prepare for old age?" he would reply: "Eat right, exercise, don't smoke, and select long-lived parents." Now, however, he adds, "Take charge of your life."

Zarit said he was very surprised at research results (cited in Barker, 1997) that showed a take-charge attitude is the critical point. This research followed 142 men and women whose average age was eighty-seven. After four years they found that people in their eighties and nineties may be more likely to hold on to their health if they feel in charge of their surroundings. "People who cope with life in a more active way seem to be able to compensate for the changes that occur in very old age," Zarit reported (p. 1C). The research examined how people who remained independent differed from those who needed help. The researchers thought that poor health would be the whole story, but they found that it was people's own psychological resources that made the difference.

Marilyn Albert (cited in Restak, 1997) of Massachusetts General Hospital and Harvard Medical School, has tested thousands of older people over two decades. She has discovered four factors associated with enhanced brain function and healthy brain aging, the last of which she believes to be most important:

- *Education*—produces neuronal connections
- *Strenuous exercise*—increases blood and oxygen supply to brain by maintaining the health of the blood vessels connecting heart to brain
- *Enhanced lung function*—increases oxygen in blood stream from lungs to brain
- *Self-efficacy*—taking control of one's life and destiny

Depression-related factors play a large part in undermining a person's sense of control, and social interaction is critical. Stamina, related to resilience, courage, and pioneering spirit, means increased staying power in the face of misfortune, and the ability to change and function effectively when stressed, which is imperative for robust aging. For the most part, stamina in later years is the result of successful adaptations earlier in life (Restak, 1997).

"Stamina in later life is contingent on a triumphant, positive outlook during periods of adversity," according to psychologist E. J. Colerick (cited in Restak, 1997, p. 121). "Persons who view situations involving loss as threatening, overwhelming, and potentially defeating experience no such outcomes: low levels of stamina mark their later years." Colerick emphasizes the importance of attitude and positive orientation as determiners of stamina.

Personality also plays an important role in practicing mental prowess. A sense of self-efficacy may protect our brains, buffering it from the harmful effects of stress. According to Marilyn Albert (cited in Greider, 1996), evidence indicates that elevated levels of stress hormones may harm brain cells and cause the hippocampus (a small seahorse-shaped organ that is a crucial moderator of memory) to atrophy. A sense that we can effectively chart our own course in the world may retard the release of stress hormones and protect us as we age. Albert concludes that it's not a matter of whether or not a person experiences stress, but his or her *attitude* toward it. This should encourage older people to maintain their independence for as long as they can, even if their health may be deteriorating. Up to a point, a high sense of mastery may make up for an increase in frailty.

CHAPTER TWO

Aging as Mental Decline

Shattering the Myth of the Shrinking Brain

The human brain does not shrink, wilt, perish, or deteriorate with age. It normally continues to function well through as many as nine decades.

—Alex Comfort

The brain is designed to function for a lifetime. The idea that age automatically brings decline in mental ability—that if you live long enough the brain breaks down and senility is inevitable, a fate escaped only by a few lucky ones—is a myth. Yet it is one of the most prevalent and generally accepted myths in our society. Pioneers in the field of aging are beginning to shatter this pervasive belief.

Leonard Hayflick, a biologist specializing in aging at the University of California Medical School, for example, states, "The old idea that senility is a normal accompaniment of aging is simply wrong. This realization has become more significant to our understanding of the normal aging process than any recent laboratory discovery about the aging of the human brain" (1994, p. 165). Zaven Khachaturian (cited in Greider, 1996), director of Alzheimer's Associates' Ronald and Nancy Reagan Research Institute, says "there's no reason to expect [the brain] to deteriorate with age, even though many of us are living longer lives" (p. 43). And Comfort (1981), perhaps a bit more blunt than the others, says: "Old people become crazy for three reasons: Because they were crazy when they were young, because they have an illness, or because we drive them crazy—and the last reason is more common" (p. 4).

It is important that we begin to see the myth of aging as inevitable decline for what it is—a myth—and move on to a productive attitude toward aging. We should heed the words of Betty Friedan, who says: "The view of aging as inevitable decline constrains psychologists' ideas about the limits of human capacity, constrains employers' ideas about the age limits of productive work, and constrains everyone's ideas about the limits of our own personal growth" (1933, p. 222).

Age and Brain Size

We have been told that we lose ten thousand brain cells (neurons) every day from the age of thirty on, and consequently, since they are not replaced, we will one day run out! This rate of loss of neurons would amount to about two billion in thirty years, which is about one-seventh of an ounce of an organ that is more than two pounds total. Actually, we have a "brain reserve"—one hundred billion neurons with a trillion connections in each cubic centimeter, firing ten million billion times each second—all comprising an infinitely complex chemical factory (Henry,

1996). Moreover, when some cells die, others close ranks and take over, rather like an army that loses soldiers but regroups and keeps fighting.

New imaging techniques such as positron-emission tomography (PET) and magnetic resonance imaging (MRI) have given researchers a more accurate picture of what happens to our brains as we age. Dr. Marilyn Albert, a psychologist at Massachusetts General Hospital, confirms that "the brain does gradually decrease in size as we get older, but not at the rate we thought. We used to think that you lost brain cells every day of your life everywhere in the brain. That's just not so. You do have some loss with healthy aging, but it's not so dramatic and is in very selective brain areas" (cited in LaCroix, 1997, p. 7).

Dr. Stanley Rapoport (cited in LaCroix, 1997), chief of the neuroscience laboratory at the National Institute on Aging, agrees. The brain from ages twenty to seventy shrinks in size about 10 percent; however, this has little effect on cognitive abilities because the average brain can compensate for a lot of the loss. In measurements of the blood flow through the brain, which reflects neuronal activity, Rapoport found that even when the reaction time was the same for the younger and older groups, the groups used neural networks that were significantly different. Rapoport also reported that the older subjects were using different internal strategies to accomplish the same results in the same time. In other words, old people and young people may simply use different parts of their brains to perform the same mental task. The mature brain works differently and has ways of compensating, but it can be just as efficient as, and sometimes better than, the young brain in organizing and analyzing information.

Research is showing that our brain retains its capacities for normal, even superior, functioning well into the eighties and nineties. Normal aging does not bring the loss of large numbers of cells, particularly from the cerebral cortex, where our most elaborate thinking occurs. Brain processing during the sixties and beyond does not follow a downward curve. Also, as we age we retain considerable control over how our brain functions, and we can take practical steps to improve brain performance over our entire life span.

Neurochemistry in the Aging Brain

Hayflick (1994) briefly explains some basic neurochemistry in the aging brain. On one end of the central cell body of each *neuron* (brain cell) is a tangle of branching fine strands called *dendrites,* which carry impulses to the neuron. On the other end of the cell body is a strand called the *axon,* which can carry enormous amounts of information to other parts of the brain and to distant muscle cells. *Neurotransmitters* are the chemical messages neurons use to communicate, creating a connection, or *synapse.* In the fraction of a second, each neuron can interact with ten thousand others. Unlike other cells, they do not divide and do not deteriorate with usage or wear and tear, but perform better and more effectively with increased activity. The concept of "use it or lose it" is based on this unique quality of human neurons. Stimulating the mind with activity and mental exercise causes neurons to branch wildly to communicate in tag fashion with each other. The branching causes millions of additional connections. In some parts of the aging brain, the synapses, or contact points, are missing or altered. However, "to this day a connection between decreased mental function and brain cell loss has not been proven" (p. 163).

Healthy brain activity in later years depends on the healthy functioning of fifty or more neurotransmitters, the chemicals that convey information throughout the brain from one neuron to another. The problem is not the loss in number of neurons but the thinning out of the dendrites, the parts of neurons that act as receivers for impulses from other neurons. Restak (1997) uses the metaphor of a tree. In full summer bloom, the tree has the greatest number of small branches and leaves; the same tree in winter, however, has fewer branches and leaves. This is analogous to neurons in the young and the old brain. There may be a thinning out with age, but the major branches are still intact. Research with animals indicates that this thinning may not be inevitable. If the learning environment for animals is enriched, the brain retains its plumage of richly interconnected neuronal connections.

There is an ongoing debate among researchers in the field of aging over whether the aging of brain cells, or senescence, is caused by hostile elements in the environment or is dictated by genes. A recent two-year investigation sponsored by the National Institutes of Health and published in the journal *Science* found that the genetic contribution to an older person's intellect is "about fifty percent, with the balance attributable to education, stress exposure, occupations, socio-economic status, geography, nutrition, disease, and all other environmental factors that shape life" (New York Times Service, 1997a). The effect of genes on aging has long been assumed to have a high relative importance in shaping a person's intelligence. However, this influence declines over the years because the other determinants of intelligence—experience, motivation, and so forth—increase as a person ages.

"Aging is not all downhill. Older people have skills and abilities that beat most young people by a mile," according to Claudia H. Kawas (cited in Henry, 1996, p. 11), associate professor of geriatric neurology at Johns Hopkins. She maintains that aging brains hold larger vocabularies, command a greater understanding of written material, contain more ability to reason, and, overall, display more wisdom—meaning good judgment based on experience.

The increased activity of using the brain can very likely delay Alzheimer's disease symptoms for years in some adults.

The more educated are less likely to show symptoms of the disease, since intellectual activity definitely develops surplus brain tissue that later can compensate for tissue damaged by disease. Recovery from strokes is much faster, and even though parts of the brain are gone, new message routes can be created to get around the roadblock and resume the function.

It is critical to understand that the potential for cell growth never disappears in the normally aging brain. The maturing brain remains capable of learning new information and taking up new activities. "Intellectual decline in old age is not necessarily irreversible" (Schaie, 1996, p. 281). You can teach an old dog new tricks, but you have to apply new or different methods, since the mature brain learns in different ways.

Flexibility of the Brain

Current research is showing that the brain is much more plastic and fluid than was previously thought. Flexibility—that is, trying new ways of doing things—is the prime predictor of mental vivacity in later years according to Schaie (1996). Rigid adherence to routine and low satisfaction with life are associated with earlier deterioration of the intellect. Schaie reports that those who are flexible at midlife tend to experience less decline in psychological competence with advancing age than those fairly rigid at this life stage. His findings cast at least some doubt on the inevitability of general intellectual decline for all individuals.

The brain works a lot like a muscle—the more you use it, the better it works. Scientists in the past believed that the brain's circuitry was hardwired by adolescence and inflexible in adulthood. However, the ability of the brain to change and adapt is apparently with us well into old age. Research has opened up an exciting world of possibilities for treating strokes and head injuries and warding off Alzheimer's disease.

People who slow down after retirement may speed up their move toward the grave, according to Schaie (1996), who has been involved in research on adults and their mental performance at Pennsylvania State University. Schaie strongly encourages older patients to take on intellectual challenges, and reported seeing adults in mental decline begin to regain abilities with the advent of mental stimulation. He stresses that "intellectual decline in old age is not necessarily irreversible and that formal intervention strategies are available that might allow longer maintenance of high levels of intellectual function in community dwelling older persons" (Schaie, 1996, p. 281). He advocates that these techniques be moved from the laboratory to a broader social context since they are not generally known or practiced.

Every year the research information load about older adults and their mental ability is doubling, and it is reversing the stereotype of irreversible and inevitable brain decline. Animal research suggests that the more we use our brain, the more efficient our intellectual muscle gets. The brain is an extraordinarily plastic and adaptable organ, responding actively to a novel environment by growing new connections to greet it (Livermore, 1992; Scheibel, 1996).

Age and Decline in Mental Abilities

By far the most sophisticated thinking machine known, the adult brain massively outperforms today's best supercomputer. It processes billions of operations a second. There is no decline in intelligence because of age. No research correlates mental decline with healthy aging, nor proves that job performance is worse with age (Levin and Levin, 1981). However, most people (as questioned by Harris in 1981) believe that people over sixty-five are not very bright or alert and that intelligence decreases with age.

Schaie (1996) reports on an extensive study that dealt with five measures of psychological competence known as *primary mental abilities:* verbal meaning, spatial orientation, inductive reasoning, numerical ability, and word fluency. Various combinations of these abilities are represented in all meaningful activities of a person's daily living and work. Findings were that, on average, there is a gain in all the primary mental abilities until the late thirties or early forties, followed by stability until the mid-fifties or early sixties, and a loss of small magnitude until the mid-seventies. No participant had declined on all five measures, even by the age of eighty-eight.

Researchers in this study asked the group to rate their performance in the five areas. In three areas, those over the age of seventy were the most negative about themselves. However, after testing, their scores were actually *higher* than those of younger people (ages twenty-nine to forty-nine years) on two scales. Older adults may have trouble with one skill and then lose confidence and begin to feel worse about their overall abilities. They frequently underestimate their mental abilities, but their mental alertness potential is better than they think. Even though some faculties may slow down in later life, we know that older adults compensate in other ways to make up for this change of abilities.

Longitudinal studies conducted in Seattle (cited in Schrof, 1994) and Baltimore (cited in Hayflick, 1994) over the last thirty-five years with more than six thousand people from ages twenty-five to eighty-eight mirror similar results. They found that most people retain strong mental skills until age seventy, and over 25 percent of the participants continue on well past that age without a significant drop in brain power.

Harvard University psychologist Douglas Powell (cited in Schrof, 1994) described a study showing that nearly one-third of individuals enjoy a steady lucidity throughout their twilight years. He tested 1,583 persons between the ages of twenty-five and ninety-two in math and reading comprehension and in remembering a string of random numbers and found that on various tests, one-quarter to one-third of the subjects in their eighties performed as well as younger counterparts. The lowest scorers suffered fairly modest declines that did not interfere with daily living. A small number of optimal agers had exceptional scores that ranked them near the top in mental abilities for all ages.

Psychologists have known for over a century that aging people frequently process information more slowly, but the degree of difference has been exaggerated. Many older people show a fall-off in performance on tests measuring rapidity of response involving memory, reasoning, knowledge, and fluency. This decline would only be an issue in a job in which rapid and rigid timed responses were critical. As we age, a balance should be achieved between the time required to maximize speed and the care needed to maintain a high level of accuracy. For older people, errors may increase as time shortens. However, the brain can be trained through memory-enhancing techniques and continuing mental activity to collate more information faster, and to access it quicker and better.

Living longer directly relates to having a healthy brain. Keeping brain cells and circuits active prolongs the brain's optimal functioning for the full length of our natural life span. If the brain doesn't function normally, the health of the other organs will be negatively impacted and certainly the quality of survival will be affected as well.

Thomas Perls (1995), principle investigator of the New England Centenarian Study, found that people in their late nineties or older are often healthier and more robust than those twenty years younger. He concludes from the findings that the oldest of the old were indeed in better shape than has been previously assumed.

Barring health problems, the state of our brain during the mature years determines how long we will live. The Dutch Longitudinal Study Among the Elderly (cited in Restak, 1997) followed 211 Dutch people aged sixty-five to eighty-four years over an eight-year period. In those who were seventy or older, the greater the decline in mental functioning, the shorter the life span. The investigators concluded that the "rate of decline of cognitive function is an independent predictor of longevity in older persons. This rule is valid even among people with Alzheimer's disease—the worse the mental impairment, the shorter the life span. Thus all of us face the same challenge: if we fail to employ our brain in varied and challenging ways, our very survival is threatened" (p. 246).

Richard Restak (1997), a neurologist, neuropsychiatrist, and clinical professor of neurology affiliated with George Washington University Medical Center and author of several books on the brain, asserts that, contrary to popular belief, the brain of an older person is not inferior to that of a younger person—it is just organized differently, with unique strengths that compensate for the slowing that inevitably accompanies aging. We can sustain our mental activity as we age by maintaining physical health through exercise and good nutrition, compensating for reduced energy levels, cultivating our social life, and developing new intellectual interests. Restak also stresses the importance of treating depression and changing our lifestyle, which may protect us from dementia.

Marion Diamond (cited in Hopson, 1984), who conducted a series of interviews with active elderly people who were over eighty-eight years of age, offers these comments:

> I found people who use their brains don't lose them. It was that simple. These people were interested in their professions even after retirement. They kept healthy bodies . . . other denominators were activity and love of life and love of others and being loved. Love is very basic. (p. 70)

For future direction, Diamond advises treating older workers with greater dignity, essential at any age. She emphasizes that we must "combat the negative attitude toward the aged, the idea they can't learn" and she stresses changing our attitudes toward retirement. "I prefer to think of retirement as changing, going in another direction, not removing yourself from life or work altogether," she says (p. 70). The main factor is stimulation, and the brain can be active at any age.

All current research strongly emphasizes that mental and physical activity is essential. It's use it or lose it. For the majority of people who do not develop a brain disease, a decline in intellect is not an inevitable part of aging.

Age and Memory Loss

Why can't I remember things like I used to? This thought whirls through the mind of most adults as they search for their keys, checkbook, phone numbers, names. The myth that memory failures are a natural part of the aging process and nothing can be done about it is closely related to the myth of the decline of mental ability. Scientists are increasingly questioning how much memory loss is attributable to "normal aging" and whether it can be reversed or even prevented. Although such research is in its infancy and much more work needs to be done, some scientists feel that age-related memory loss could possibly be eliminated in our lifetime.

In general, as we get older, we do experience a decline in the ability to "make new memory"—that is, to take in new information rapidly and establish new knowledge, especially when we are under pressure to do so. However, aging does not affect all types of memory evenly. According to an article in the *Harvard Health Newsletter* (Elias, 1992), "semantic remembering—general vocabulary and knowledge about the world—shows little decline until the seventies. But after thirty-five, it's more difficult to retrieve names, especially those used infrequently."

Meanwhile, this loss of memory, the mental capacity that changes most in the mature brain, is a major fear of aging adults. Changes in "tip of the tongue" and proper names memory, which are somewhat adversely affected in normal aging, do not actually interfere with normal functioning. Memory changes occur but are limited to the rapid acquiring and retrieval of new information, and these decreases in performance can be made up for by memory training. Brain neurons do not die off in droves, nor do they shrink or go dormant, according to Gerald Fischbach at Harvard University (cited in Schrof, 1994). The healthy mind's storehouse remains intact but may be a bit more difficult to get to in old age. Just as running the latest software on an older computer takes more time, one can have first-rate intelligence but lose some speed and accuracy on cognitive challenges later in life.

Age-associated memory impairment (AAMI), not related to Alzheimer's, strikes 38 to 50 percent of those between sixty and seventy-eight, and little is known about its development. Most researchers discuss free radicals, the body's waste molecules that wear away at the brain cells and cause an impairment in memory (Chen, 1997). These tend to start in middle age and range from difficulty in remembering names to serious gaps in recall.

Many people believe that there are proven antiaging drugs for preserving and enhancing the brain. Currently, pharmacological agents to reverse memory loss in normal and pathological aging are in various stages of testing in mammalian models, and some have advanced to human trials. Because of recent advances in research on mammalian models of learning and memory, there is, in the next decade, the prospect of providing drugs to older adults to aid their learning and memory processes.

The reality is that today, all antiaging drugs for the brain are in the research stage, with many studies especially focusing on preventing Alzheimer's, not enhancing mental powers. Much research is being conducted on what happens to brain cells when their power begins to fade, and this work may eventually lead to a wide range of chemical approaches to preserving and enhancing cognitive function.

According to James L. McGaugh (cited in Greider, 1996), who has worked on memory-enhancing drugs for forty years, there has been evidence in laboratory animals that recall is enhanced with drugs as well as hormones. But he cautions that we are still a long way from safely and accurately fine-tuning the brain with chemicals. "The first generation of memory-improving drugs may be a breakthrough, yet their effect may be modest" (p. 44). Restak (1997), like most serious researchers, concludes that it will be years before a "safe dependable drug is available for rejuvenating the brain and reversing age-related cognitive changes" (p. 227).

So, while sales have gone up on many of the supposedly anti-aging products for the brain, many renowned neuroscientists like Khachaturian liken the use of these products to the superstition of tossing salt over your shoulder. Although research is being conducted with promising results, most neuroscientists who work with drugs believe that, for most people, the way to maintain high brain function will not be found with chemicals. As McGaugh (cited in Greider, 1996) stresses, "There's growing neurobiological evidence that supports the common sense notion of 'use it or lose it.' The brain may be more a muscle than we ever thought" (p. 70).

The Role of Education in Brain Functioning

All life should be a learning experience, and we know that education enhances brain function, stimulating the neurons in our brain. Native intelligence may also protect our brain. Smart people may start life with a greater number of neurons and, therefore, have a greater reserve to fall back on if some begin to fail.

"If you have a lot of neurons and keep them busy, you may be able to tolerate more damage to your brain before it shows," according to Dr. Peter Daniels of the Albert Einstein College of Medicine in the Bronx (cited in Greider, 1996).

Researchers (Chopra, 1993; Restak, 1997; Schaie, 1996) seem to agree that of all the factors contributing to successful brain functioning in the later years, education may be the most important. In a study sponsored by the National Institutes of Health under the leadership of Gerald McClearn at Pennsylvannia State University (New York Times News Service, 1997a), a group of 240 male twins were given intelligence tests as armed forces inductees in the early 1940s. Fifty years later they were retested. Results showed that cognitive performance in early life predicted cognitive ability in later years. Those with the highest measure of intelligence and most extended education showed the least cognitive deterioration with aging. It is likely that more education, higher intelligence, a larger brain, or more synaptic contacts provide greater cognitive reserve, thus allowing the mature brain greater tolerance for injury. The role of heredity in cognitive ability appears to increase with age, not decline.

Khachaturian (cited in Restak, 1997), says: "Education creates more synaptic connections and enriches the dendrites. Since it takes longer to reverse these changes, those with better education stay mentally alert longer than those with less learning" (p. 115). A survey of the research shows there is little doubt that continuing education and learning enhance the brain's reserve capacity through their effect on brain structure and function. You learn a new skill by modifying the organization of your brain. Each time that skill is used, the brain circuit is activated, and when you stop, it slows. Practicing mental skills compensates for aging changes by not allowing disuse to occur. Practice builds up reserve capabilities either by maintaining neuronal circuits or by establishing new ones. The more you use your brain, the greater the protection against the incursion of brain disease and aging.

As we age, curiosity about the world and stimulation from increasing knowledge and insight enhance the dendritic connections. Because of the different amount and quality of stimulation, two brains with different numbers of neurons and neuronal connections will age very differently. We have choices and can seek experiences that promote mental and physical stimulation and contribute to the enhancement of our brain.

Unlike our genetic makeup, over which we currently have little control, we can actively further our education and learning as a protector against mental decline. It's important to realize that stimulating education does not have to involve the accumulation of degrees and structured time spent in the classroom. Cultural experiences at any age can compensate for limited educational opportunity earlier in life. For strongest positive effect, it is important that we value and enjoy what we are learning.

General knowledge about the world continues to increase until very late old age ("Keeping Your Brain Active," 1997). Those in the second midlife may be able to capitalize on a lifetime of learning and experience, becoming better at interpersonal relationships, drawing on what they know about others.

Education is a lifelong process that, through brain modification, confers antiaging benefits. As our brain performance improves as a result of learning, we generally feel more empowered and more confident. Achieving mastery over a body of knowledge is highly confirming. Getting and staying on a learning curve is critical and can involve many activities later in life, including the challenges of entrepreneurial success.

Job Performance and Age

The changing demographics will increase the number of older workers, and questions will increasingly come up regarding their productivity as the early retirement of the recent past decades begins to change. Interest in the relationship between aging and work behavior will increase.

Salthouse and Maurer (1996) summarize the research that evaluates job performance and career development. They found, as they say, rather surprisingly, that there is no direct relationship between age and ability or between ability and job performance if the latter is determined by KSAO (i.e., knowledge, skills, abilities, and other factors). Considering that there is some decline in abilities—for example, immediate memory and complex reasoning—why is there not a negative relationship between age and job performance? This seems puzzling and is a critical question needing more research. Cognitive ability has been found to be one of the best predictors of job performance. This would clearly seem to lead us to believe that there is a negative relationship between age and job performance, but such a relationship has not been documented. Perhaps this is a result of limited data—only thirteen studies plus some additional recent ones are reported. And very few studies have focused on examining age relations in managerial and professional occupations (p. 356). Another problem is that the studies have not compared samples with employees in their fifties and sixties. General mental ability and job experience are the two most critical individual determinants of job performance (Schmidt and Hunter, 1988). Since some factors of mental ability are negatively related to age, but job experience is usually positively related to age, the natural question would be, What is the overall effect?

Researchers are in agreement that older workers have been reported to have lower rates of absenteeism, fewer accidents, and higher levels of job satisfaction than younger workers. Salthouse and Maurer (1996) speculate that perhaps "the overall values of the older workers to the employers may be equal or possibly even greater than, that of the younger worker" (p. 358).

In trying to separate myth from reality, the research is focusing on several questions: Which tasks actually show decline with aging, and which are spared? The focus is on *explicit memory*, which requires an intention to remember and then yields an awareness of having done so, and *implicit memory,* which does not involve a conscious recollection of remembering. Age may impair explicit memory, but implicit memory is not affected.

Can the memory performance of older adults be significantly improved or maintained, and if so, how? Hultsch and Devon (1990, p. 267) address this critical question. They say that domain-specific improvement in memory performance could be done. The interface between cognitive and social processes is complex. The cognitive processes do not operate in isolation from personality and social processes. Competence and performance are different. Three variables are important determinants of performance: (1) knowledge of what the task requires and strategies that may be applied—know-how; (2) motivational factors such as expectations, sense of self-efficacy, and attribution about outcomes—desire and self-confidence; and (3) personality variables such as traits, states, and stylistic modes of perceiving and responding—personality and work style. Research has focused on the first two and suggests substantial age differences in some areas but not in others. Age differences in the area of self-evaluation of cognition appear to be substantial. In particular, older adults tend to perceive themselves as less efficacious on many cognitive tasks as compared to younger adults or themselves when they were younger (p. 268). If older adults kept on a conscious learning/growth curve, they would have more confidence, and this would not be the case.

Much of the work has been framed within two hypotheses that are more psychological issues than biological. One suggests that deficiencies in self-knowledge (e.g., of task demands, of strategy, selection of monitoring performance) might be a major source of production deficiencies on many cognitive tasks. The other hypothesis suggests that poor self-evaluation (low sense of self-efficacy, lack of sense of control, inappropriate performance attributions) results in lowered effort and consequent poor performance. In other words, it's our beliefs creating our biology. As George Burns used to say, we think ourselves old!

The Brain and Disease

The brain represents where we live in our personal life; our very identity—personality, memories, and soul—are found here. In the words of Michael Fossel (1996), professor of clinical medicine at Michigan State University: "in a fragile quart and a half of jelly is where aging often becomes a tragedy; here we lose ourselves" (p. 135). While heart disease is the cause of most human ailments as we age, Alzheimer's disease and senility represent the worst of our fears about aging. Much is still unknown about these conditions, although they are currently the subject of continuing research.

Senility and Alzheimer's—classified as *dementia*—are not the inescapable fate of the elderly. Dementia, now the fourth most common cause of death in the United States, is a disease and a distinct *pathological process*—that is, a sign that the brain is not normal—not the consequence of aging.

Sapolsky (1992) explains how stress can contribute to dementia. He says that stress causes the adrenal gland to create steroids that are damaging to the neurons in the hippocampus, the brain's memory area. They die when the steroid levels are high. These hippocampal cells in turn also are part of a system that turns off the adrenal gland's stress response. So a vicious cycle begins: the more stress experienced, the less the adrenal gland has a working mechanism to turn it off, thereby creating more damage. Consequently, the more stress, the more lost neurons, increasing the risk of dementia.

A highly recommended way to keep your mind healthy and prevent Alzheimer's disease (AD) is taking the necessary steps to reduce the risk of stroke, which strikes five hundred thousand Americans annually.

When a stroke damages the brain cells, there has been no way to revive or retrieve them. However, a surgeon in Pittsburgh, Douglas Kondoziolka, is beginning to use a highly experimental procedure—drilling a hole in the skull of the stroke victim and injecting millions of laboratory-grown, immature nerve cells. It is hoped that these cells will survive, make new connections and restore lost brain power (cited in Fackelmann, 1998). Much very similar research is being conducted at the University of South Florida College of Medicine in Tampa. Researchers are optimistic that their expected results will help victims of strokes but also a wider variety of conditions. However, at this time the jury is still out.

A research project focusing on more than seven hundred elder Catholic sisters labeled "The Nun Study" (cited in "Preventing Alzheimer's Disease," 1997) has revealed much information about the aging brain. The sisters, who live an average of eighty-five years, have devoted their brains at their death, but meanwhile they are being observed and studied by David Snowdon, a professor of preventative medicine at the Sanders-Brown Center on Aging at the University of Kentucky. So far they have found that even one or two very small strokes in susceptible areas of the brain that may have no detectable or lasting symptoms can trigger AD or worsen its symptoms. They also have found that those who earn college degrees, who teach and constantly challenge their mind, live longer than the less-educated nuns who clean rooms and work in the kitchen. Snowdon hopes to prove that the better-educated sisters have more cortex and more synaptic branching of neurons than those less educated, which would stave off dementia and stroke.

Autopsies have shown that sixty-one of the nuns had the abnormal "tangles" in the brain that characterize AD. Nearly half of those with autopsy-detected AD also had oxygen-deprived areas of the brain characteristic of stroke, even though they weren't diagnosed with AD while alive. The nuns whose brains showed evidence of both stroke and AD were eleven times more likely to have had symptoms of dementia while alive than those with no evidence of a stroke. Conversely, those with brain evidence of AD but not of stroke were less likely to have overt AD symptoms. The kind of strokes suffered by the nuns were ischemic strokes caused when a blood clot in a brain's arteries deprives an area of oxygen. The good news is that the damage from this kind of stroke can be prevented. It's recommended that suspected strokes be treated as a brain attack with all the emergency of a heart attack. Although there is still much to learn about dementia, there is room for cautious optimism. About 50 percent of the researchers in this area feel Alzheimer's and other brain diseases can be prevented. Although dementia does increase with age—20 to 40 percent of eighty-year-olds exhibit some signs of it—a healthy brain that shows none of the signs of dementia will continue to function normally for a lifetime.

How to Keep the Mind and Memory Sharp for a Lifetime

Friedan (1993) sums up the message on aging and mental decline: "Much research has shown that the most important predictors of vital age are satisfying work and complexity of purpose" (p. 222). Below is a checklist of suggestions for keeping the mind and memory sharp for a lifetime:

- Use it: Stretch your brain, keep learning and thinking to build your brain circuitry—most researchers support the commonsense notion of "use it or lose it."

- Know and achieve your major life goals.
- Focus on doing things that you believe make a difference in life and that provide you with a purpose.
- Become actively involved learning something diverting and unfamiliar.
- Work puzzles, learn a musical instrument, fix something.
- Try the arts.
- Exercise (a strong relationship exists between exercise and blood flow to the brain).
- Meet and interact with intelligent, provocative, interesting people.
- Seek variety and a broad range of experience.
- Be flexible, improvise, and try new things and new ways.
- Find peace—be kind to yourself! Shake off negative attitudes, depression, anxiety, anger, and discontent.
- Take courses that you enjoy, but don't cram.
- Develop expertise using high levels of thought.
- Make friends.
- Seek challenges but avoid burnout.
- Seek new horizons and novel experiences.
- Avoid constant routine to keep your mind limber.
- Attempt to keep control over your life as much as possible.
- Follow but question the scientists and sages, and watch out for the snake-oil salesmen with new chemical antiaging approaches.
- Investigate the prescription and alternative remedies that have some basis for validity: vitamins E and C, estrogen (for menopausal women), perhaps ginkgo, antioxidants, choline.
- Avoid harsh and continual stress and learn to relax and practice meditation.

- Take your time, practice mindfulness.

- Pay attention, concentrate on what you want to remember.

- Minimize and resist distractions.

- Use a notepad, carry a calendar.

- Seek out and use humor; lighten up, take time to focus on fun!

- Organize belongings; have a place for unforgettables—for example, put a car key in a magnet and hide it on your car, keep a secret outside door key.

- Repeat names of new acquaintances in conversations.

- Take care of your health, eat well, exercise, and take steps to avoid chronic diseases such as cardiovascular disease, severe hypertension, arthritis, tumors, and osteoporosis.

- Nurture and cultivate long-term relationships with well-educated and intelligent people.

- Maintain a meaningful occupational status with workplace complexity.

- Realize that retirement is a positive factor only if you are retiring from a routinized job, but not from a highly complex job.

CHAPTER THREE

Aging as Decline in Creativity

Shattering the Myth of Wilting Originality

To be creative means to consider the whole process of life as a process of birth, and not to take any stage of life as a final stage. Most people die before they are fully born. Creativeness means to be born before one dies.

—Erich Fromm

The need for creativity in their life and career is my clients' major underlying motivation for re-careering. However, they may not initially label it as such because creativity is too often narrowly defined as connected only with producing art. In reality, it can include any or all of the following:

- The capacity to be puzzled

- Awareness

- Spontaneity

- Adaptive flexibility
- Divergent thinking
- Openness to new experiences
- Disregard of boundaries
- Abandoning
- Letting go
- Being born every day
- Ability to toy with the elements
- Gusto (relish) for temporary chaos
- Tolerance of ambiguity

This is a partial list of the forty characteristics of creative people, according to symposia held at Michigan State University in 1957 and 1958 (McLeish, 1976). The fourteen participants, whose goal was to define *creativity* or the *creative process,* included Rollo May, Margaret Mead, Erich Fromm, Abraham Maslow, and Carl Rogers. Age was not identified as a consideration in these meetings. However, for decades gerontologists and researchers, based mainly on a study by Lehman (1953), have accepted with little question the idea that creativity declines after age thirty. The many well-known public figures who have produced long into old age have been either ignored or explained as aberrations.

What is clear today is that there is no arbitrary age cutoff for superior human accomplishments—they can span the entire lifetime, and can develop and accelerate in the later years. Many artists, leaders, and familiar personalities reached their most productive peak in their later years. Michelangelo designed St. Peter's dome when he was nearly 90 years old; Anna May Robertson ("Grandma") Moses began painting in her seventies and lived to age 101; Katherine Graham was awarded the Pulitzer Prize in 1998 at age 80 for her autobiography; Mark Twain, after suffering severe family and financial losses, took to the Chatauqua trail, found a new audience, and paid off his debts in his late seventies, writing what some consider to be the best American satire. The list goes on: Winston Churchill, Ray Kroc of McDonalds, Colonel Sanders of Kentucky Fried Chicken. All their stories are well-known in our culture, but dismissed as being the exceptions and therefore not applicable to the "average" adult.

In my own practice, I have watched many of my clients achieve high creativity in their capstone career—their best yet—quite late in life. Whether dictated by circumstances outside themselves, an "aha" personal insight, or a systematic career planning process, people are finding a worthy means of fulfilling themselves. Late bloomers are "growing up" or "finding themselves"—an unpredictable and creative process. Blooming late in the season is a natural, but not an easy or automatic, process.

Often it is not until midlife, when we are free for the first time from the conventional workplace box and parenting responsibilities that have required time and attention, that we actually discover and release our creativity for the first time. Creativity does not wilt or drop off automatically with our age and, based on the experiences of many of my clients, it can actually flourish at midlife, perhaps for the first time. An example is Gene Murray, an excellent public school teacher who had taught music, computer literacy, speech, and drama, and acted in and worked on an annual outside musical production each summer. Facing the opportunity to retire from his teaching position in Canyon, a small town in west Texas, he decided to explore his options. He wrote that he wanted me to guide him to a "new and exciting career for my second time around!"

His need to further his creativity was evident. He researched becoming a teacher abroad, or a social director on a cruise ship, but they weren't quite right, so he explored other options closer to home. His recent e-mail on his current activities is on page 64.

MYTH BUSTER : GENE'S OPTIONS

I am teaching computer-generated music at Amarillo College on a half-day basis so I can still receive full teacher retirement. I am assistant artistic director of Amarillo Opera and did the stage directions for our recent performances of *Carmen*. It was a huge success. I am also costume designer and "general flunky" since I can tailor men's costumes, paint sets, do the choreography, and sing roles. This is one of my dearest loves: opera!

I am also composer-in-residence for Amarillo Opera. We have performed nine of my operas, and two more are in the works. I just found out that our trumpet teacher at Amarillo College has chosen a trumpet sonata and a trumpet/two soprano trio I wrote, to perform on this faculty recital in May. Everywhere I turn there are wonderful thrills!

Just to keep cobwebs from growing on me, I also direct the Interscholastic One-Act Play at White Deer, Texas. This is a tiny little town where the students are really serious and hard workers. I travel sixty miles one way three times a week and have a really good time with the students. I'm also a full-time granddad and husband, so I'm not bored very often.

Thought I'd let you know there's a half-page announcement of my opera *Wage of Sin* in the last edition of *Opera America.* If you don't have access to the publication, send me your fax number and I'll fax you the page. This sixty-three-year-old is pretty excited. They don't choose many composers and one can't pay his way in, so that made it doubly exciting to me.

Gene, a free agent well into his second midlife, is thriving in his capstone career. On a follow-up questionnaire, these were his answers to some of the questions:

Q: What do you like most about your new career path?

A: I'm in complete control and using all my creative talents.

Q: What do you dislike most about your new career path?

A: Not enough time to do everything I want.

Q: What were the greatest barriers to overcome to make your career change?

A: To believe in myself. To give up a monthly check.

Q: What resources were most helpful to you in making your career change?

A: The Career Design process made me realize I was only as limited as I believed I was.

Q: What have you gained by making a career change?

A: Complete freedom! I do what I want, when I want.

Q: On a scale of 1 to 5 (1 = minor; 5 = radical), rank the degree of your career change.

A: 5.

Q: What advice would you give to anyone considering making a career change?

A: Go for it!

Gene's a creative success at later midlife, and so are countless others. Perhaps part of the misperception about creativity lies in its definition, since creativity is a "nebulous concept that does not lend itself to easy scientific assessment" (Simonton, 1990, p. 121). In evaluating assertions that creativity declines with age, we must look at how creativity is being defined and measured. It is questionable whether standardized assessments such as paper-and-pencil tests can be used to measure creativity. Furthermore, creativity as a characteristic may exist only as potential that can perhaps be developed and released as one goes through certain life experiences and cannot be measured.

If we have a narrow definition of creativity, limited only to artistic production—a painting, poem, design, a song, or an invention—we are cutting off its main roots. Cole and Winkler (1994) point out that creativity "often results in less tangible outcomes: the altered self-image of an individual or group; a change in how one lives; the deepening of a long-term relationship; a more acutely felt intuition of one's place in the family, in a religious group or in nature" (p. 6). They also point out that creativity can be our most profound response to the current loss of certainty, and that being deeply involved in a creative action can carry us through the debilities of time passage.

From my point of view, creativity involves a five-step process:

1. Taking the known or familiar pieces (of a life, a design, words, thoughts—or whatever)
2. Shaking them out of their existing patterns
3. Filtering them through one's unique experience and mind's eye
4. Instinctively seeing a new pattern
5. Selecting the pieces and arranging them into a pattern that didn't exist before

This is exactly the process I use in helping people change careers at midlife—the most challenging creative process imaginable. Finding a new career involves creating a future identity based on matching inner needs—motivation, traits, values, and skills—to the realities of the outer world. We must plow through the accumulated multiple layers of conventional expectations, mindless assumptions, stereotyped beliefs, and nameless "shoulds" and "oughts" and learn to trust our own instincts and intuition. This is a creative process that can come with age if we actively pursue it.

Creativity in living a satisfying life in today's very uncertain world is a major challenge but necessary. It involves creating our own life and seeing it as a process of growing and becoming. As we add years to our life, we will add new experiences, insights, ideas, knowings, mysteries, questions, and quests. If we view life as a continuing upward journey, accumulating experience, creativity, insight, and wisdom, our aging can be seen as the most critical part of it: the final strokes of the paintbrush that create our masterpiece. Aging is a creative process that involves risks and difficulties along with the continuing joy of discovering insights and concepts today that were outside our awareness yesterday. With this attitude, our world will expand, not shrink or decline with age.

Carl Jung (1933, 1977), despite his admitted fear, broke out of his traditional academic career at midlife and moved into the unknown to identify and create innovative spiritual psychological concepts. Jung felt that our preoccupation with youth inhibited our spiritual and psychological growth in later years. From his many patients who suffered feelings of anxiety and meaninglessness, he learned that they looked back and clung to the past and carried with them the fear of death.

Maslow (cited in McLeish, 1976) discusses two elements of creativity. One he calls *special talent creativity,* the creativity of the gifted inventor, poet, novelist; and the other he terms *self-actualizing creativeness,* which involves changes in the personality such as responding to life's challenges and problems. This self-actualizing creativeness, the kind of creativity Yeats was referring to when he said, "It is myself I remake," involves choice, self-confidence, and belief in what one is doing. The blocks to this kind of creativity include fear and lack of will, confidence, direction, and energy.

I believe that the desire and the potential to create is inherent in all of us, but it develops in different forms and from varying sources and at different ages. Much of the frustration and meaninglessness experienced today are caused by limited vision or limited ability to tap the sources of creativity—or perhaps we are mindlessly waiting for "permission." We certainly cannot fulfill this kind of creativity if we define it too narrowly or are forced to measure it inappropriately.

Marvin is an example of someone who was able to accomplish the incredible based on his creativity and commitment. He achieved full tenure position and associate professor level at Baylor Dental School at the chronological age of sixty-five, following his career change from a full-time dental practice to teaching and writing seven years earlier.

A highly creative poet, amateur actor, and teacher, Marvin, who was an excellent professional, was not a typical dentist. This became a real problem when he developed serious irregular and rapid heartbeat episodes stemming from the continuing detailed and annoying administrative duties of his large practice, a strong mismatch for his best skills.

Marvin's career assessment scores indicated he was highly creative, with writing, teaching, and counseling as his focus. Dentistry as an interest was not showing up, though his skill level in it was high. Teaching at a dental school was a natural—combining all his dental training and actual practice experience with his more natural aptitudes and interests. He applied, waited a few months, was called, sold his practice, and moved to a new life. Marvin acknowledges his pain in making the change was high.

Creativity, Marvin discovered, was the major element missing from his earlier work, and he defines it as a matter of wanting to do things a little differently, not necessarily following everyone else's pathway, but creating his own path, knowing that for himself and for the people he is creating it for, it's going to be better.

His attitude is open and flexible. He meets regularly with other teachers to share what they're teaching, and he acknowledges this learning is very important.

He also acknowledges that the change was scary, and he did have to overcome his own fear of change. In our follow-up, he stated that the level of fear he experienced in making the change was a "4 on a scale of 5," but that "if you don't take the step, you dote in misery for the rest of your life. It's scary because you go from the known—like an old pair of shoes—to the unknown." Marvin says he is "so happy he made the change; there is absolutely no regret—I would never go back!" He has no second

MYTH BUSTER : MARVIN'S CHOICE

I was scared to death. Going to the dental school initially involved a huge cut in income, and I wasn't sure how I would fit in. I was giving up a known entity to go to something unknown. In spite of that, I knew I had to do it. Once I got settled in, I could not be happier.

I enjoy what I'm doing. I can do what I'm supposed to do, and I feel that they must want me there. If any one of those conditions is not met, I'm gone—nobody is going to have to tell me. Right now, they're all being filled. I'm very happy. I don't have any plan or specific date for retirement. If I do drop full-time, chances are pretty good that I'd go part-time for a while, unless . . . I find something else I want to do, and then I'll change careers again.

thoughts about his career change, in spite of the decreased income, which has climbed considerably, though not where it was originally. And he is alive, happy, and well.

Marvin says that his payoff is the creativity and recognition from his work. He doesn't want awards or medals; the recognition comes in the tenure, the promotion, and the salary. When they give an increase slightly above the average salary increase, he considers this special recognition. And when he's asked to be on a committee or task force, this is a compliment, recognition that he's a person who will get the job done. If they want him there, he'll do the very best that he can. In his second midlife, Marvin is now getting what he wants from his life and work.

In his personal time, Marvin has taught a creativity workshop to adults and has written and published two books of poetry. He performs his haiku (an unrhymed verse form of Japanese origin) at bookstores throughout the state with a friend who plays the Japanese flute. What does writing haiku give Marvin? "It allows me in a very short form to express many thoughts that

MYTH BUSTER : MARVIN'S SUMMARY

Creativity is the spice that makes the flavor of joy jump into the recipe of a person's life. Without creativity, life can be bland, unrewarding, and sometimes distasteful.

Joy is the ingredient in life that neutralizes stress. When joy is not present, stress overcomes and chisels away at the integrity of one's psyche and soma, eventually causing the imbalance called illness. This imbalance serves as a signal to take inventory and reassess to find out what is needed to reestablish the balance called good health: physical, mental, and emotional.

For over thirty years, I established and maintained a successful professional practice. As the years went on, joy diminished and stress increased until the day the imbalance appeared in the form of depression and an irregular, fast heartbeat. The time had come to reevaluate; with help and wise counsel, I left my practice to become a teacher of aspiring dental professionals.

For me, working in academia has provided many opportunities for creative enterprise and for sharing from my warehouse of experience. The joy took an upswing and the stress became motivating instead of destructive. The increase in creative endeavor was the spice that now makes life not only more palatable, but more productive to me and to others.

I wasn't even aware I had." Marvin wrote the above summary on creativity.

Marvin's story, similar to those of countless other clients, validates that creativity, rather than declining with age, can emerge and grow. It was waiting to be tapped and released. The process of recognizing and tapping into this source requires breaking through the misinformation and myth that cling relentlessly to our current aging model and taking action steps to follow through.

PART TWO

Learning a New Way to Tell Time

The newly aging are overwhelmingly seeking opportunities in their work for growth, control, creativity, direction, and flexible options. Contemporary role models actually demonstrating these qualities in the work world have seemed conspicuously absent until recently. Instead, there are currently countless messages reflecting cynicism, alienation, stagnation, conformity, and entrapment—all predictive of decline, disaster, and death.

At any age, whatever suggests a downward slope, a lack of growth and learning, or a falling away increases the negative sensitivity to aging. Growth keeps us alive, living a life in which our inner self and external reality interact to produce a sense of challenge that, when met, produces new, additional challenges. This is a continuing process of connecting and integrating the value of growth and aging. Emphasizing continuing growth regardless of chronological age fortifies the tendency to delay the long declining prologue of death—aging. While growth doesn't stop the chronological time clock, it keeps us from becoming psychologically old in the decaying sense.

Successful aging and working will require revising and updating our current model and expectations to fit new realities. Our new second midlife age, sixty to eighty, has traditionally been seen as "old." This is a view that will now be shifting dramatically. Our expectations of age have been determined by the characteristics of those now elderly, quite dramatically different from those of earlier generations. We will soon have the healthiest and the most formally educated population between forty and eighty of any era. Aging and working for this group will pose different problems for them and for society, and this is certainly happening now.

My clients at midlife are searching to know and express their talents, to connect with their creativity, and to know that what they do matters. They want to leave some mark. Success without this is hollow and meaningless. Becoming an adult of age, creativity, and purpose requires that we refocus on functionality rather than chronology, keep on an active and adventurous learning curve, rethink retirement, and cultivate our wisdom.

Part Two explores the major challenge at our second midlife: to forget the bell curve of up, plateau, down, and out, and to continue to shape a new self in our rapidly shifting environment—in other words, learn a new way to tell time.

Focusing on Functional Age

Chronological age is an unreliable measure of aging—but a proven measure of the passage of time called birthdays and receiving presents.

—Leonard Hayflick

"Knowing what you know now about yourself and the world, what would you do with your life and in your work if you could deduct twenty years from your chronological age?" This is the major question I present to my midlife clients as they redesign and enhance their career. The critical challenge is to free ourselves up so we can determine the answer to this question and then devise a successful action strategy to achieve it, or a close version of it.

A major step toward becoming a person whose creativity, wisdom, power, and purpose develop with age is to learn a new way to count time. Why are we suddenly supposed to be old at age sixty-five? What is the critical scientific evidence for this?

There is the story, perhaps partly fictional, that we owe this to the German Chancellor Bismarck, who in the 1870s (when the German life expectancy was forty-two years) engineered his rise to power by observing that his rivals, all federally employed, were over the age of sixty-five. Seizing upon this, he allegedly masterminded legislation to retire all public servants who had reached that age, whereupon he ascended to power with ease.

In the 1930s, when the U.S. government was establishing the age for receiving social security benefits, sixty-five was adopted as the age for retirement. This was a time when life expectancy was around forty-five and the unemployment rate was 25 percent. How mindless can this be for today's workforce, with life expectancy at seventy-eight and rising rapidly, and unemployment at its lowest level in twenty-five years? It is as if at this age some mysterious biological event occurs that makes humans old at the stroke of midnight.

Following the dictates of chronological age slams the door on successfully integrating our age and worklife. In all my research, *not one expert in the aging field says that chronological age is a reliable measure of our actual aging.* It is an accepted convenience only.

I became concerned about the fear of aging and its impact on adults and their careers after working for twenty years with clients making career changes. In almost every case, hesitation and fear in making a career change that they strongly believed essential to their emotional and financial welfare was accompanied by genuine anxiety about advancing years in general. Even clients in their thirties and forties saw their age as a major barrier in making a career realignment.

Dispelling fears about aging and reexamining outdated conscious and unconscious stereotypical beliefs of aging is a critical first step in redesigning a career.

Biological, Social, and Psychological Aging

Aging is generally defined in biological, social, and psychological terms. *Biological aging* relates to basic processes that range from cell physiology to the whole organism's physical health status. In terms of biological aging, we resemble a clock shop rather than a single clock—all the tissues and organs ticking at a different rate. As Hayflick (1994) suggests, knowing our biological age would have more meaning than knowing our chronological age, but we can't know our exact biological age because of the variations of the ticking clocks of all of our body organs. Different parts of the body are in fact different ages. At a certain chronological age—seventy, for example—your body will be like no one else's in the world; its age changes will mirror your unique lifestyle.

Social aging refers to changes in role positions and social functioning. We start school at five, get a driver's license at sixteen, become a legally responsible adult at twenty-one. In contemporary urban society we have the notion that a precise chronological age marks the transition from one stage of life to another, which is highly questionable. For example, having babies by age thirty, a dictate of previous generations, has certainly altered. Today, the chronological ages of twenty-one and sixty-five define the lower and the upper boundaries of participation in the adult world, as well as the cultural definition of full humanity. Unfortunately, as it is today, those over sixty-five have no defined active roles in our society. So what are we to do with our highly extended long life?

Psychological aging is concerned with patterns of changes in emotional, cognitive, and mental functioning as people mature and grow older. Chronological age as a marker of organism growth and psychological development is at best imprecise (Birren and Schroots, 1996). Psychological age is flexible and personal—no two people have exactly the same psychological age because no two people have had exactly the same experiences. How old you feel you are has no boundaries, and can reverse in a split second. Recently a client in a career crisis said he felt seventy-five years old; before the crisis he had felt forty, and his chronological age was fifty-four.

When gerontologists try to predict longevity, all of these factors—biological, social, and psychological—must be taken into account to accurately determine if the aging process is being accelerated or retarded. Instead of coming up with a fixed answer to the question "How old are you?" we need to arrive at a sliding scale that shows how fast our different ages are moving in relation to one another and then put them together in a functionally aging package—how we actively function at this particular time in our life.

Chronological Age

Chronological age refers to the number of years, months, hours, and minutes that we've breathed. This is an outdated but strongly established system that maintains tight control over our destiny. Yet there is absolutely no expert on aging today who holds that chronological age is a preferred or valid way to determine our actual age. Eminent biogerontologists assert that aging is not merely the passage of time, and that time itself produces no standardized biological effects. Hayflick (1994) maintains that "events occur in time, not because of its passage. The biological events that follow birth happen at different times and occur at different rates in each of us" (p. 13). For gerontologists, aging is chronological only in the legal and social sense—for example, birth certificates record the number of years that have elapsed since our birth. "In an increasingly rationalized, urban industrial society, chronological age came to function as a uniform criterion for sequencing the multiple roles and responsibilities that individuals assumed over a lifetime" (Cole, 1992, p. 3). Yet all this is beginning to change and will do so with increasing momentum, so that former chronological models become passé.

We must break the mind-set that chronological age, the age on your birth certificate, is your real age. Our increasing longevity, emerging with improved nutrition and fitness, better medical services, and scientific breakthroughs in the prevention of disease, might lead us to expect midlife to start at sixty and not forty. However, because of our social and cultural expectations, we program ourselves to begin to fall apart at a certain designated age, and we oblige.

Ryder (1965) has suggested that old age be arbitrarily defined as the point in a group's life span when the expected remaining years of life is ten. Frankly, with our ability to stay healthy, I see that old-old age should be the time when we have approximately three years left to live. Neugarten (1986) proposed that older age should be at least divided into the *young-old* and the *old-old* because the service delivery needs, health, and functional limitations of these groups diverge widely. Although the exact age for this boundary differs among investigators, the old-old in the past have often been defined as seventy-five years and above, although more recently the oldest-old have been defined as eighty or eighty-five years.

If we need some kind of aging chronology, I suggest we design our own. The following is my "live long, die fast," contemporary model for aging:

Young adulthood: 20–40

First midlife: 40–60

Second midlife: 60–80

Young-old:	80–90
Elderly:	90 and above
Old-old:	2–3 years to live

A major problem for aging adults is that frequently their health issues are seen by themselves and their doctors as inevitable aging problems and left untreated. Though chronological age is limited as an indicator of physiological decline among humans, physicians commonly associate certain diseases with old age, or age-related health in a patient. Having a much younger but physically out-of-shape doctor examine me and declare, "you're in better shape than I am" is not reassuring or helpful. In dealing with our health, Comfort (1976) gives us some advice: if you "find someone who thinks that in the natural order you have to be infirm, crazy, impatient or the like, by virtue of chronological age, change doctors" (p. 67).

It is not how old you are, but how old you think you are and how old you function that is important. Furthermore, exercise can reverse ten of the most typical effects of biological age, including high blood pressure, excess body fat, improper sugar balance, and decreased muscle mass. According to Chopra (1993), elderly people who adopt better lifestyle habits improve their life expectancy by ten years on average.

Teaching older adults life skills can also significantly benefit health and quality of life. According to one study (reported in "Health News," 1997), adults aged sixty and older living independently who participated in group and individual life-skills sessions for nine months (where they learned about nutrition, exercise, public transportation, and how to adapt to their changing abilities) fared better than those who were involved in only social activities or no program. This indicates that people are able to learn and adapt as they age.

An individual's rate of aging may vary significantly from what might be predicted from the averages. There is no single aging process or general pattern of aging applicable to all of our organs. Aging results from the highly individualized interaction of genetic, environmental, and lifestyle factors, but all reliable research studies emphasize that the disabilities frequently associated with old age are caused more by the effects of disease than by the aging process.

According to Restak (1997), society is shockingly remiss about how we treat our older citizens based on their chronological age. Older people are actually more diverse than any other age group, and grouping and labeling them in the same category is highly misleading. One person can lose functional capacity before age sixty-five and should be retired. However, no com-pany would close a productive plant, so why retire people who are capable of innovation and creativity? What about "the Picassos who can function creatively into their 90s? Society should stop making decisions about a person's usefulness on the basis of age and start making those decisions on functionality" (p. 78).

Functional Age

Since it's impossible to know our precise biological age, and since chronological age is not a reliable base for making critical decisions, I seriously urge my clients to forget chronological age and focus on functional age. How well do we perform, educate, actuate, execute? How capable are we of operating to fill our designed needs or in achieving a utilitarian and fulfilling purpose in our life and world? Functional age combines and integrates the biological, social, and psychological measures into one active package. It allows us to look at our own aging straight on and to get reality-based objective information for beginning the process of shaking ourselves loose from our fear of aging.

Jack Nicholson, now in his sixties after nearly sixty films, is the image of the genuine antihero, the alienated rebel who never quite surrendered. His presence suggests that he knows the score and is beating the aging system at its own game. Not thrilled about the idea of birthdays, he says flatly, "I ignore them, I started in 1972 to simply eliminate the calendar. I don't record things by days or weeks. Oh, sure, I know I can't play juveniles anymore. But there are new kinds of parts that I've never played before that I can play now" ("Jack Nicholson Interview," 1997). This is successful aging—moving on to new parts and roles.

According to a study by Taves and Hansen (1963) of 1,700 older residents of Minnesota, 40 percent first considered themselves old at age eighty or older, 13 percent said they never thought of themselves as old, and only 5 percent thought of themselves as old at sixty-five. Apparently, actual chronological age for some people over sixty-five has little to do with seeing themselves as elderly.

This denial of aging could be labeled a form of avoidance, but it is not necessarily a negative approach. It is used by many in the attempt to avoid aging's negative stereotypes. A positive form of avoidance for the aged is to reengage—substitute new roles for old roles lost—perhaps through remarriage or full-time or part-time jobs, paid or volunteer. Older people who are in good health and remain socially active may continue to feel strong and vigorous, whereas those who are socially uninvolved, isolated, or disengaged tend to classify themselves as old.

Garson Kanin (1978) tells about a meeting with Laurence Olivier, then in his middle fifties. Recognized as one of the greatest actors of the century, Olivier had played all the important leading Shakespearean roles, acted in many contemporary and classic plays, directed and produced films and plays, and had become a movie star. However, Olivier was tired, and there were small but significant signs that his career might be fading. Undaunted, he told Kanin, "I'm going to have a smashing third act!"

During the next fifteen years, Olivier made his most impressive contributions to the theater, with great performances in *King Lear, The Dance of Death, The Entertainer, Becket,* and *Othello.* His directing talents led Great Britain's National Theatre to glory. While acting and producing and administering this superlative theatrical organization, he planned and supervised the construction of the new National Theatre.

We, like Nicholson and Olivier, can ignore the calendar years and stop the chronological clock from relentlessly ticking. What if we subtracted our probable extra twenty years from our present chronological age? What would we do today, knowing what we know now about ourselves and the world, if we were twenty years younger? When you know the answer to this question, then go and do it. Move on with your life. Take action. Forget who or what you are supposed to be because you are a certain chronological age.

Staying youthful involves forgetting chronological age and focusing on functional age. This message must be actively and continuously reinforced during the entire career refocusing process. This message is not merely an inspirational one, but one based on research and information. As the conventional belief system about oneself and the aging process loosens, shifts, and fades, additional career choices and options will emerge.

Summary

If you didn't know your age, how old would you be? The important thing is the age we act, perform, execute, move, think, feel—the age at which we function. When I pose this to many of my clients who have been genuinely frozen in their thinking about their future career direction, it's amazing to me how rapidly they can name what they would do and be! Without realizing it, our

T A B L E 1	*Ten-Step Formula for Successful Aging and Working*

1. Age functionally—not chronologically.

2. Stop your aging chronological clock at whatever age you are now.

3. Take control of your second midlife, your extra twenty years of good health.

4. Insert this twenty years now at your midlife—don't add them to your old age.

5. Subtract these twenty years from your current chronological age for your possible functional age.

6. Visualize what you would do if you were that age, knowing what you know now.

7. Design a strategic action plan to accomplish this.

8. Go and do it, or some close version of it!

9. Grow and become a person of age, wisdom, creativity, power, purpose, passion, and pursuit.

10. Live long, die fast! Be "old-old" a shorter time.

chronological age can unconsciously and automatically block our thinking about our future. Table 1 summarizes my ten-step formula for successful aging and working in the twenty-first century. We grow old, not by living a certain number of chronological years, but by becoming idle in mind, body, and purpose. We decline and decay by abandoning our flexibility, our ideals, our talents, our life's mission, and our involvement in our community. We grow old and retire by buying into society's story that we can be surplussed, junked, and discarded.

We are told it's time to grow old, and others expect it, and we defer and play our part. The most deadly assumptions related to aging are that retirement and old age are directly connected to the chronological age of sixty-five, that mental decline begins at age twenty-one, and that senility is inevitable if we live a long time. We all know people who were old and stale at thirty, with underdeveloped mental and emotional powers, and others who at eighty-five were actively and creatively growing and producing. What this means is that we can ignore chronological age and focus on functional age. This is what I teach my clients to do as they prepare for their capstone career.

Laurence Fagg (1995) points out that we created the clock and now it's our master. In the past there was only the sun, moon, and stars, and what the priests and prophets lacked in scientific precision they made up for in intuition and spiritual insight. My belief is that today people don't need a clock as much as they need a compass to keep directed.

When a role ends for one part of our life there is another role waiting. Socialization to a new role requires clear expectations, however, and possible incentives. A role as an elder or senior citizen must carry the same respect as any other role in adulthood. Levin and Levin (1981) believe that something must be in it for the aging to give them a sense of usefulness in a society where usefulness is valued.

I am not opposed to clocks—as a matter of fact I collect them, dozens of them. I'm intrigued by all kinds, and I'm surrounded by them. But only infrequently, when my clock repairman makes a house call, are they all set and running at the same time. I do have a healthy respect for time as a resource to use wisely and thoughtfully, but not as a preestablished system to mindlessly control our life. Reserve or throw out all the old notions of what you must do because of a set chronological age and what it means to "act your age."

CHAPTER FIVE

Following the Ulyssean Way

... you and I are old;
old age hath yet his honor and his toil
Death closes all; but something ere the end,
some work of noble note, may yet be done,
... tis not too late to seek a newer world.

—Alfred Lord Tennyson, *Ulysses*

For today's man or woman at midlife seeking a role model for a satisfying and meaningful life and work direction, I use the very human hero Ulysses, the Latin name for Odysseus, as best personifying the qualities we can emulate and relate to in the second half of our life. Ulysses was an illustrious leader and a warrior who plays a rather minor role in Homer's *Iliad*. He leaves his beloved wife, Penelope, his father, and his infant son to fight in the Trojan War, not realizing that it would be twenty years before he returned. At the war's end, he begins what becomes his ten-year journey home, the story of Homer's *Odyssey*. Though Homer probably lived in the eighth century B.C., this work describes heroic acts of his past that may have happened around the twelfth century B.C. Ulysses was probably between fifty and fifty-five years old at the beginning of his journey home—very old for that time.

Everyman's Journey Through Life

Homer's recounting of the arduous wanderings of Ulysses during his ten-year voyage home is literature's grandest evocation of everyman's journey through life. Ulysses' reliance on his wit, wisdom, and wiliness for survival in his encounters with divine and natural forces is at once the human story of an individual test of moral endurance.

On his way home, Ulysses is shipwrecked but rescued by the beautiful nymph goddess Calypso. Smitten by him, Calypso wants to marry him, and her promise is, "Stay with me and you need never grow old." The illusion of immortality or regaining youth through a younger partner is not an uncommon temptation faced in midlife, and this may be especially true for men. Loyal to Penelope and homesick, Ulysses refuses her offer of sex and immortality. However, Calypso detains him for seven long years hoping he will change his mind. She is finally ordered to release him by the god Hermes, but she foretells the trials and tribula-

---

I credit my Ulyssean model to John A. B. McLeish, who wrote *The Ulyssean Adult: Creativity in the Middle and Later Years* (published in 1976 and updated as *The Challenge of Aging* in 1994). McLeish is a Canadian scholar and teacher who worked in the education of adults in the mid-1970s. This book was ahead of its time and was out of print and unavailable when I first read it in the late 1970s. It was republished by the Ulyssean Society, an active group spawned by the influence of this teacher, who died in 1995. An informative memorial Web site is located at www.centennial.qc.ca/jvarey/mcleish/default.htm. McLeish's books, and also a newsletter, are available from The Ulyssean Society, 215 Richview Avenue, Toronto, Ontario M5P 3G2, Canada.

tions that await him on his voyage home and repeats her offer. She says, "if you only knew deep down what pains are fated to fill your cup before you reach the shore, you'd stay right here, reside in our house with me and be immortal" (Homer, 1996, p. 36, 5.228–31).

Again he refuses: "Much have I suffered, labored long and hard by now in the waves and war. Add this to the total—bring the trial on! . . . So let this new disaster come. It only makes one more." Ulysses sees himself as having no way to go but up. "And what if the powers above do wreck me out on the wine-dark sea? I have a heart that is inured to suffering, and I shall steel it to endure that too. For in my day I have had many bitter and shattering experiences in war and on stormy seas" (p. 159, 5.244–48). Ulysses has no illusions about the value of taking the easy way out or living forever.

Ulysses makes a difficult but wise decision to move toward his future and not dwell on the sorrows or glories of the past—a demanding choice that many in our second midlife cannot resist. Under his extreme trials he could have given up by suicide or by simply relaxing momentarily his constant vigilance, resilience, and determination to keep himself alive. Under constant strain and weariness we can be tempted to take a shortcut or let things slide; and under some circumstances, even death may seem preferable to the unending physical fatigue and emotional strain many of us face in our adult life.

Ulysses could have also given in to yet another temptation— the singing Sirens, perhaps the greatest temptation of all. The strength of the Sirens' appeal was that they sang irresistibly of all his pain and his past glory and heroic feats in the war—all that a new generation, even his family, would have little interest in hearing. In other words, no one would really be interested when Ulysses told his war stories.

He could join his war comrades, the heaps of lifeless corpses around the Sirens, and relive the saga of his past (or the bingo, shuffleboard, and soap operas), or he could forgo living on the glories of his past and head into an unknown, uncertain future, focusing on his destination. He chooses to move forward, but wisely has himself bound to the mast of his ship so he can resist temptation. Later, he never mentions or recounts his past war battles to Penelope or his son Telemachus. How many of us in our second midlife spend our energy recalling our past glories? Ulysses forged ahead—so must we!

Continuing on his journey home, all is calm and serene at first. But then, as Calypso predicted, disaster strikes. The god Poseidon, his enemy, seeks revenge with a storm so powerful that "Ulysses' knees shook and his spirit quailed." The craft goes down and Ulysses must strip off all clothing and swim for two days and two nights. Using all his strength, courage, shrewdness, and common sense, he reaches the shore, almost dead. He lay there, "naked on the shore," grimly facing his plight. Most of us, certainly by our second midlife, have come to this point, "naked on the shore," seemingly stripped of all except our self. Only at this point do we, like Ulysses, drop our ego defenses and become our genuine authentic self. Only when faced with hardships can we discover the source of our strength for the last half of our life. Sheehy (1998) has found that men especially have great difficulty in making the changes necessary for transitioning at midlife. Some actually have a physical blowout or a mental plunge into depression before they can give themselves permission to change.

When disaster and defeat occur, we must begin new adventures to rebuild our fortunes as Ulyssean adults. We must find our essentially life-loving, resilient, striving natures and be open to the possibility of creativity and growth. When we hit bottom, we have no place to go but up!

The type of creativity and courage evoked by the depths of despair or disaster is what Maslow called "self-actualizing creativeness"—how we respond in our personal life to the blows of fate. Resiliency, coming alive with a transformed vision, a new gift of sight, is the Ulyssean adult's creativity in action.

Of course, there are other choices. We could give in to self-pity—the "poor me" syndrome. Or we could choose to live more cautiously and avoid risk at all costs. As McLeish (1976) puts it, we could "play it safe: move back into all the comforting conventions of routine life," and live a life of "total expectedness" (p. 237). While there can be good sense and value in the routine, if combined with passiveness and maintained too long, routine can engulf and enslave us. Furthermore, merely riding the routine may not be an option in today's chaotic work world.

Just as the hero Ulysses continued to thrive and make new voyages when he was older, so should we continue to live positively and creatively throughout our entire life's journey. Life should be a process of continuous creative growth, especially in the later years. The ability to learn is fully operative through our entire life span: creativity is not limited to geniuses, but includes thousands of manifestations of the mind and imagination that transform an individual's own self or environment.

Following the Ulyssean way in the latter part of life means rising above the deficits and decline and having the courage to look life directly in the face, not turning away. In this way, life will not be the sad downhill journey of decline that is accepted by many, including gerontologists and others in the medical profession. The extra twenty to thirty healthy years that have been bestowed on us are a gift only if we use them wisely and creatively. Our second midlife can be the most creative, courageous, committed time of our life if we determine to make it so. However, there's no promise that it is necessarily an easy journey.

The Ulyssean Factors

Ulysses is a model for successful contemporary aging in our rapid-fire, changing age of information and technology. As portrayed by Homer, Ulysses is remarkably complete and larger than life, an all-too-human hero embodying every characteristic of a complex human individual. What are the Ulyssean factors we can initiate and follow as we age?

Anderson (1970) defines the Ulyssean factor as the human need for adventure and exploration. It's the survivor factor present in all but highly developed and indestructible in some, compelling them to firsthand discovery. *Courage* is the most striking quality evidenced by Ulysses in his drive to return home and his search for new experience, regardless of his age.

Self-sufficiency also characterizes the Ulyssean way. But this does not necessarily imply being a loner. Self-sufficiency involves the readiness to rely on one's own efforts and to go it alone, though not to the exclusion of working with others.

An overwhelming *need to know* is most characteristic of Ulyssean adults, and this frequently drives them far beyond the normal limits of human fatigue and aging. All bodies tire, but Ulyssean adults' combination of self-discipline, courage, and determination enables them to be tireless in their drive to understand and accomplish!

Ulyssean adults frequently take to adventures of *self-exploration* characterized by openness of mind, sensitivity to the need for new ways and new experiences, resourcefulness, courage, curiosity, a continuing sense of wonder, and genuine humanness. They accept factors of aging but are not intimidated by them. There is a consciousness of the quest for the self through life's drama.

Sometimes at midlife, adversity, not success, is the force that drives us to the Ulyssean way. Misfortune presents choices: we can accept defeat quietly or launch into creative planning and action, using our imagination. McLeish says that of all Ulysses' qualities, the one that makes him unforgettable is not so much his capacity for success as his *intense humanity and intrepidity in the face of failure.* Though a heroic leader, failure and loneliness were his frequent companions, no less terrifying because so often sent by forces he could not control: the capricious and hostile gods from Olympus. In the same way, few of us who have lived a full life have escaped its hardships and disasters.

We must work to gain *creativity*. McLeish (1976) says, "Obsolescence of mind and spirit waits for those who think that creativity in later years descends like manna from the sky." To bring it all together requires great "exertion of the self—exertion undertaken with love, faith and hope" (p. 247). Ulysses on his odyssey discovers the truth about himself and his relation to the gods, a key to creativity and growth, and finally returns home, a greater man for all. On the other hand, James Joyce's two characters in his novel *Ulysses* can't discover the key to their loneliness and frustration, and consequently their potential for growth is forever stunted.

The small creative adventures, as they multiply, fill life with a certain verve and get us ready for larger odysseys. What holds us back from them is the image of what we think we ought to be. We feel we need to follow the rules of a work world that may still be in the industrial age or society's dictates of the face of later years and old age. It "isn't done" or it "can't be done" are the words that constrain us. Small Ulyssean performances lead to great ones. In later life, the role of the will and of creativity are paramount. If we are to follow the Ulyssean way, we must accept the reality of change, not passively and reactively, but imaginatively and dynamically to create change for ourselves and society.

Moving Forward

It is not easy today to follow the Ulyssean way, to break free from all our immobilizing blocking forces—lack of confidence, grief of lost expectations, fear of failure, loss of nerve, fear of the unknown, physical decline. We can begin by setting up little odysseys. Ulysseans know that advancing years bring hazards; like Ulysses, they could be "naked on the shore" because of forces over which they have no control. They look directly at the face of their life, not away from it; and as McLeish (1976) says, they "cultivate the high art of looking at both the human comedy and the drama of the mysterious universe with intense interest and wonder," and foster in themselves the conditions that promote creativity: "freshness of outlook, spontaneity of feelings, acceptance of the constructive disorder of change, loving respect of the past" (p. 286). They don't fret about their inevitable declines and deficits, and they have a deep awareness of the future based on a clear, calm eye focused on the present. This is creativity for successful aging in action.

I use Ulysses as a model because he retains the questing spirit for adventure and growth both in the exterior world and in his interior self, translating it into a new way of seeing, understanding, and doing. He has the courage and resourcefulness for continuing renewal through tragic adversity and deep disappointment. We, too, can use our failures as the forces that drive us into wholly unexpected ventures. Our misfortunes present us with new chances and opportunities.

Elders who moved forward late in life abound despite the myth of aging as decline. Thomas Hardy, credited with being our first modern English novelist, gave up novel writing and began writing poetry at age fifty, and did so until his death at eighty-five. Maggie Kuhn, with her great strength of will and drive, when forced into retirement by the Presbyterian Church, joined with other retirees and created the Gray Panthers, working into her late eighties. Will Durant started the ten-volume *History of Civilization* after age fifty-eight, and worked on it through his eighty-ninth year. Benjamin Franklin, at a time when the life expectancy was thirty-three for men, was seventy in 1776 when he sailed to France (where he won the heart of more than one

Frenchwoman) to enlist its aid in the American Revolution. At seventy-five he negotiated the peace, and at eighty-one he saved the Constitutional Convention. Edith Hamilton at ninety-one received the highest public award in Athens for her work *The Greek Way,* written after she retired as headmistress at Bryn Mawr School for Girls. Cervantes, a professional soldier, wrote *Don Quixote* when he was almost sixty. Alfred North Whitehead published his four major works after the age of sixty-five. Buckminster Fuller's mind and hand teemed with innovation past age eighty. Edison never retired. Historian and author Henry Cammoger died at ninety-five, but taught classes at Amherst until he was ninety-two years old. My great-grandmother, a nurse in the Civil War, was an active midwife until she died at the age of ninety-four.

Our culture is full of Ulyssean adults who are creative and contributing as long as they live, starting ventures at late midlife and creating until death. These are our models for a new way to age and work in the twenty-first century. You can compile your own list. "Life," said Ben Franklin, "like a dramatic piece, should not only be conducted with regularity, but methinks it should finish handsomely" (cited in Kanin, 1978).

One of my clients, Mary Jane, dared to seek and discover the Ulyssean way. Originally she was a discouraged and burned out middle-aged public school teacher with a physical disability. She was depressed because of countless family problems, and these were compounded by working in a school with a principal who wanted her out of the way. Mary Jane was fighting a losing battle to keep a job in a hostile, negative environment. She talked initially about escaping education altogether and moving into the business world, a choice that did not fit her background, skills, and personality in the least.

Initially, we relieved some pressure by getting her transferred to a different school for a year while coming up with her options. Beneath Mary Jane's conventional exterior was someone desperately, almost irrationally, longing for adventure and excitement, some escape from the boredom of a barren west Texas town and her continuing family problems. She dreamed of writing children's books, of travel, of a world she had never seen except in her imagination. It would have been easy to ignore this need from someone who on the surface had so few options, to convince her that this was an impossible dream that she should forget.

We searched for options and carefully filled out her application for a teaching job with the Department of Defense. Within the year she was offered a teaching job in Germany for two years. She made new friends immediately, received top evaluations for her teaching, and traveled with other teachers all over Europe in her time off. After two years, she was transferred to Japan. She reported that she was taking notes and pictures, and planned to write books to help children understand and accept other cultures. Often we dare not even verbalize our aspirations and give up too quickly on our dreams. Mary Jane was well into her capstone career when I last heard, a change that was not easy but was able to materialize with a little direction and encouragement.

CHAPTER SIX

Rethinking Retirement

Retirement is the ugliest word in the language.

—Ernest Hemingway

Compulsory retirement may be a major factor in the desire of older adults to avoid the role of senior citizen. Retirement separates individuals from previous roles, without providing them with the motivation for building a new self-concept in another role. When many individuals disengage from work, they are isolated from former co-workers, and they no longer have the means to carry out whatever social roles they formerly played. They become teachers with no students, businesspeople with no business, speakers with no audience, writers with no readers.

However much one may grumble about the hassle, our daily work is critically important to us. "Making the transition from work to retirement is one of the biggest changes we make in our lives. The key to doing it successfully is in the planning," according to social worker Nolan Brohaugh (cited in Craig,1996, p. 13).

Planning Your Nonretirement

Without a retirement plan we may make unwise choices: my sister Madolyn is an example. A painful identity crisis accompanied her retirement. She had no plan, and felt she was no longer respected and approved of by others. She saw herself instead as "on the shelf," an "old-timer," and "done for." Her way of coping was to immediately plunge into a rather mindless marriage. She soon realized her mistake, ended the marriage, and embarked on a journey of soul-searching and self-analysis to determine what to do for her third act.

She decided to use her talent for public relations and customer service to build a successful business as branch manager for a large corporation's insurance department. She wisely deducted ten years from her age of fifty-seven when she was hired, and she became their top producer before retiring at seventy.

Though chronologically eighty years old, she functions more like a traditional sixty-year-old and has found her real niche. Born with a high dramatic flair, she naturally writes and converses well. She values her role as the family matriarch. She travels to remote places, experiencing home stays through SERVAS, a peace organization. In addition to keeping in touch with her worldwide friends and handling public relations for worthy causes, she writes family history, tracing ancestors back to 1600, and records stories passed down from early family members. This family history—remembrances, stories, and memoirs that were saved from nothingness—is a priceless gift that transmits meaning and value to later generations. Madolyn doesn't plan a second retirement, but will continue juggling world tours, genealogy, public relations, and family matriarch duties. Her life is filled with endless growth and Maslow's "self-actualizing creativity."

Comfort (1976) says to plan for retirement ten years before the date, and that two weeks is about the ideal length of time to be retired. Dr. Charles Everett, my internist, who has countless patients in late midlife, quizzes them about their upcoming retirement plans. After hearing what they say, he tells them, "Well, it should take you about two weeks to go fishing, clean the garage, the attic, and rebuild the fence. What do you plan to do for the next fifteen or twenty years of your life?" Most men, he has discovered, have no idea past that point. Thomas Moore (1993), a medical writer for the Center for Health Policy Research at George Washington University, reports that remaining in the workforce, along with not smoking, is a crucial factor for longevity in men.

Adjustment to retirement, though a major predictable passage, is difficult; and the younger the retiree, the harder the transition, according to 41 percent of retirees surveyed in New York in 1993. Also, the higher the status one had at work, the "steeper the slide to anonymity."

An interview with Lee Iacocca in *Fortune* magazine (Taylor, 1996, pp. 50–61) captures what it's like to retire from a position of power with no real plan: "I really wanted to retire. I had turned sixty-eight and I was getting tired. I'd done everything." He felt bogged down in paperwork, with too much going on, and he wished to simplify his life, but he wasn't ready for retirement. "Most people aren't, especially CEOs," Iacocca said. "You can plan everything in life, and then the roof caves in on you because you haven't done enough thinking about who you are and what you should do with the rest of your life. Those guys who retire at fifty-three with early buyouts have a hell of a problem." He says that pulling up roots was the hardest part and advises others to hold on to something familiar: a house, a wife, friends. He estimates that statistically he has ten years left but plans to beat that and live twenty. Now divorced, he's alone but optimistic. He's still busy, but if he were without that work "and without my kids and grandkids, I'd lose it—I'd have nothing."

Without careful planning, compulsory retirement can and does deflate the adult's self-image, particularly when it comes at a time of a well-established social role and self-image (Bischof,

1969). Chopra (1993) says that medical and psychological issues in America and England are triggered by mandatory retirement because it sets an arbitrary cutoff date for social usefulness. One day before a worker is sixty-five, he contributes labor and value to society; the next day, he is one of society's dependents. Medically, the results of this shift can be a real disaster. In the first few years after retirement, heart attack and cancer rates soar, and early death overtakes men who seemed otherwise healthy before they retired. Chopra calls it "early retirement death," and it is created by the belief that one's useful days are over.

An interview with Ray Charles ("It's Not Over Yet," 1997), a ten-time Grammy award winner, supports the notion of nonretirement. "What would I retire to? Music is my life," says Charles. "When the good Lord wants me to retire he will take care of that. I work as much as I want." The sixty-six-year-old performer was making his thirty-seventh world tour with his sixteen-piece orchestra. "Fortunately for me, my heart is still good and I feel good, and that's the main thing. What's really the most wonderful thing in the world is doing something you love to do. Making people happy keeps you alive. Life is supposed to be meaningful."

George, one of my clients, is now well into his capstone career after traditional retirement. He has a doctorate in physics, and had pursued a rather lackluster career in engineering at a large semiconductor company for twenty-eight years. George took an early retirement at age fifty-seven, and had no clear idea what to do next with his life.

Though trained as an engineer, George was not a technical thinker. Engineering held no interest for him, and nothing in his assessment or our conversations suggested it as a match in any form. A breakthrough for George came when he recalled that at fourteen he daydreamed a lot about becoming another Robert Louis Stevenson and writing adventure stories, and he had thought of majoring in English. In fact, he told me rather reluctantly that he had written, though not published, two adventure novels already. Here is George's story.

MYTH BUSTER : GEORGE'S MOVE

I had a Ph.D. in physics, a successful career with a large semiconductor firm, a wonderful wife and family, income, security. What more could I want? A good question. In spite of all this, I knew I wanted something else but, unfortunately, I didn't know what it was.

For several years, in fact, something had been wrong—something missing. My work was no longer satisfying. I found myself dreading Monday and "just getting by" until Friday. This was not the way it was supposed to be. Although I didn't realize it at the time, my wife insists I was becoming increasingly more irritable and hard to live with. Something was definitely wrong.

Could it be a plain case of burnout? Perhaps. But how does one know when he's suffering burnout? Or could it simply be the approach of retirement time and the gnawing dread of facing an uncertain future? I didn't think this was the case because, more and more, I found myself longing not to retire but to do something different.

I began to realize I had to make some sort of move, to change to a different way of earning a living. The thought, while exciting to contemplate, was both frightening and perplexing: frightening because of the uncertainties involved; perplexing because of my lack of knowledge concerning what else I might be qualified to do. At the time, I felt too "specialized" to work at anything other than what I was already doing. Yet the thought of continuing along the same path was terribly disheartening. There had to be a better way. Something different. Something satisfying.

In the spring of 1989, my company offered a retirement package designed to tempt some of the older employees to retire before they reached normal retirement age. In addition to the pension fund and the profit sharing I had accumulated over the years, the company also was offering an "early retirement incentive," a lump sum of cash based on salary range and the number of years of service.

Tempting though it was, I didn't accept the offer. But I did begin to prepare for the next time such an offer would be made. After all, companies all across the nation were laying off and "downsizing," and I felt fairly certain mine would repeat the early retirement offer again in the near future.

With the help and support of my wife, I began to investigate what I needed to do in order to be ready the next time the offer was made. Early in the search, I noticed a course in planning for a career change offered by an adult continuing

(continued)

education organization. This looked like something I could use to get some ideas on what to do. Immediately, my wife and I both signed up for the course. The rest, as the saying goes, is history.

The course was conducted by Dr. Helen Harkness, founder of Career Design Associates, Inc. My interest was immediately sparked to take a hard look at the elements involved with a career change. I became a client of CDA and entered an intensive program of assessment and self-evaluation that began to reveal unrecognized and untapped skills. I began to realize I had some valuable talent that would be marketable to potential employers. My bruised ego began to heal and I developed a revitalized spirit of self-confidence. Where earlier I had doubted that any employer would want to hire me, now I felt I really had something to offer. As the self-evaluation continued, my confidence grew steadily. I stopped worrying about where I was in life and what I was going to do next and began looking forward to the next phase of life—whatever it was going to be.

For quite a few years, I had been interested in fiction writing and had taken creative writing classes. In addition to a number of short stories, I had completed the manuscripts on two novels. The work at CDA revealed that my self-expression was being stifled where I was working and that my need to stimulate my creativity was evidently rooted in the desire to write. A number of potential career paths, such as teaching or city planning, were examined, but the day Dr. Harkness and I first discussed the possibility of my becoming a technical writer, I knew immediately that was what I wanted to do. Any idea of doing anything else dropped completely out of the picture.

Now my new career path was clear in my mind. The choice seemed so logical and obvious that I wondered why I hadn't gotten the idea much sooner. But as Dr. Harkness explains, the decision to change careers cannot be made quickly or simply. One must go through a process of stages, much like a grief process, involving the shedding of the old and the taking up of the new, which isn't easy. It involves work and, in most cases, a certain amount of fear. But when one achieves a new career path and embarks on a new life for which one is more suited, all the work and fear is more than justified.

With my wife's full support, I excitedly began planning the next phase of my life. Sure enough, as I had expected, my company again offered the early retirement incentive package in the fall of 1989. I had another discussion with Dr. Harkness about it, and when she said she

(continued)

thought I was ready to make the change, it was as if the weight of the world had been lifted off me. I signed the retirement paperwork the very next morning, and from that day to this have never looked back nor regretted the decision.

I quickly began picking up some necessary computer skills and am now working as a contract technical writer. My income has climbed steadily and is now higher than it was with my former company. At the same time, my interest in fiction has been rekindled and I am now completing my third novel. I find that I enjoy the independence of working for different companies on a contract basis and feel that by working this way, I am establishing my reputation in the local community as a top-quality technical writer.

In looking back on my life, I am convinced that, even as early as grade school, I had an interest in writing. I truly believe the call to write was there but, for one reason or another, I chose another path. It is certainly true that my technical background prepared me well for my present career. But whatever the twistings of fate have been, I am very grateful I had the opportunity and encouragement to make a much-needed change and to enter a new career path that gives me so much more happiness and satisfaction than the former one ever did.

In my engineering career, I could not have cared less what happened on the job. I simply went and did it. I never questioned, never gave anything a second thought. Now in my job as a technical writer, I speak up and absolutely let everyone know my opinion. I care about my projects and am willing to take risks to make them work. I'm absolutely amazed at the difference in me and how I act and feel on the job.

You know something else? I will live longer now that I'm taking 100 percent better care of myself.

George has been a contract technical writer now for almost ten years. He has completed a third novel and placed it with an agent, and it holds serious promise for publication. He is now writing his fourth in his spare time. He is thinking he may cut back his technical writing job to put more time and concentration into writing novels.

As George moved into a new career, his wife, Linda, who had provided great moral support, an essential element for an adult in career change, ventured out also. She bought the retail business where she had worked for years, and has successfully expanded and renamed it "Time Well Spent," a name suggestive of their lives today! Both are busy growing and learning adults.

Financial Realities of Retirement

"Never stand on a three-legged stool" was a clear message picked up from my savvy Scottish ancestry. Yet today millions of Americans are unthinkingly using three legs—social security, private savings, and corporate pensions—as a fundamental foundation for their future. While these might have proved stable enough in the past, relying on them for a lengthy retirement in the twenty-first century could be disastrous.

Americans between the ages of forty-five and sixty-four were asked in a survey by the U.S. Department of Health and Human Services where they believed their most important source of retirement income would come from. Their answers, reported in Table 2, are contrasted with today's reality.

Today, if we are to have any measure of dependable security, we must add *work* as a stronger fourth stabilizing leg to the retirement stool. Leaving the work world at sixty-five or earlier will not be a reality for today's generations. We will need to work longer, delaying retirement to age seventy or beyond for financial reasons alone. We simply can't afford retirement. In 1900, the average person had 1.2 years in retirement; by 1997, this had risen to 17 years (Barker, 1996).

Only 10 percent of baby boomers say they expect to work after age sixty-five, yet only 25 percent will have saved enough money to retire, according to Byron Oliver, head of Cigna's retire-

TABLE   2   *Sources of Retirement Income: Belief versus Reality*

Source of Baby Boomer Income	Belief	Reality
Company pensions	45%	20%
Social security	26%	18%
Private savings	22%	33%
Other	4%	2%
Work earnings	3%	27%

Source: U.S. Department of Health and Human Services (*U.S. News & World Report*, June 1997).

ment plan division. With children's education taking their retirement money and the future of health care uncertain, if they don't keep working, they probably face a poorer old age than they imagine.

According to Russell (1993), when baby boomers start to retire in 2011, they will need an annual income of $46,000 just to match the modest $17,000 median household income of today's elderly. After twenty years of retirement in 2031, they will need $125,000 per year to match the median income of the elderly today, assuming 5 percent inflation.

Social Security

Today's social security tax rate would have to go to 40 percent by 2029 to provide the tax benefits currently promised. The social security system will continue to produce a positive cash flow until 2011, but will be exhausted by 2029 if no action is taken. With our current retirement policies, we face real financial crisis in our social security system.

In 1900, Americans lived 1.2 years in retirement; in 1997, living beyond the age of seventy, they average 17 years in retirement (Barker, 1996). Today, more than half the baby boomers will live to eighty. As the life expectancy of the average American approaches eighty years, more and more people will live twenty or more years with only their retirement income. Actually, it is predicted that ten million baby boomers will live well into their nineties; between 1980 and 1990, the number of centenarians doubled.

In 1900, 4 percent of the U.S. population was over age sixty-four; it is now 13 percent. After 2030, 1.7 workers will be taxed to pay for every pension, but now 4.5 workers are paying for one pension. "The average elderly male now is repaid all of his Social Security tax payments, plus interest, in less than 4 years of drawing it. After that, he is on welfare in exactly the same sense that a welfare mother is" (Thurow, 1996, p. 109).

When retirement age was set by Bismarck in 1891, the average German lived to be less than forty-five, and the retirement age was set at sixty-five, at least twenty years beyond the life expectancy of citizens. If we add twenty years to our current life expectancy of seventy-six, that would be roughly equivalent to saying the government pension is for those over the age of ninety-six! This may seem absurd, but perhaps no more so than what will be happening to our tax structure in the near future. No one can finance a system where life expectancy is continually rising and the age of retirement falling.

Thurow, in summarizing the reality-based conclusions of most experts today, calls our current retirement the explosive part of a volcano pushed up by demography, with the creation of a new class of people. For the first time in history, our society will have a very large group of economically inactive elderly, and no society can afford this.

Delaying retirement could salvage the pending social security financing problems. The millions of additional experienced workers would produce, in 1997 dollars, approximately half a trillion dollars of additional goods and services beyond what the national economy would otherwise produce. The taxes they would pay, and the reduced social security benefits they would draw while in the workforce, could contribute to eliminating the looming fiscal disaster if the social security system is not drastically overhauled (McRae, 1994).

Private Savings

While the stability of the first leg of our retirement stool, social security, is questionable, the condition of the second, private savings, is even weaker. A sobering reality is that at retirement, sixteen million Americans will have no savings. According to Thurow (1996), the average American family has only $1,000 in net financial assets. To equal today's retiree income, they would have to save a sum equal to eleven times their current income. Furthermore, Thurow has estimated that those age fifty-four to sixty-five and about to retire have less than $7,000 in net financial assets, and are in even worse shape. Even with their home equity, the fiftieth-percentile households of those age fifty-one to sixty-one have less than $100,000 in assets. Baby boomers are saving only one-third of what they will need to keep the standard of living their parents had. According to Thurow, three out of four can expect a crisis when they retire, since they have saved little to nothing.

The reality, according to a study by Stanford University economics professor B. Douglas Bernheim (cited in Kaye, 1995) shows that boomers must nearly triple their current rate of saving, on the average, to be able to stop working at sixty-five. For every $10,000 of annual retirement income in 1995 dollars needed between ages sixty-five and ninety, today's forty-year-old will have to have $469,000 in a tax-deferred retirement account at sixty-five, according to benefits consultant Hewitt Associates. Assuming inflation of 4 percent yearly and a 7 percent return in retirement, at ninety the nest egg will be gone. To throw off even a modest $40,000 per year in today's dollars, that forty-year-old would need $1.9 million saved at age sixty-five. A fifty-year-old, with ten years' less inflation to worry about, would need $1.3 million.

Working and saving even five years longer can make all the difference. To retire at sixty-five with $40,000 yearly, a fifty-year-old earning $65,000 now with $50,000 saved would have to start setting aside 37 percent of earnings. This is optimistically assuming a yearly 4.5 percent raise, an employer contribution of 4.5 percent of salary and a 10 percent return before retirement. Working until seventy, the burden drops to 16 percent, about half of the earnings.

The reality is that Americans simply don't save enough. The British, Italians, French, Germans, and Canadians save more than 10 percent of their after-tax income, while most Americans save only 5 percent, far short of what is needed for a comfortable retirement. More alarming, almost 40 percent of American households have no retirement savings at all.

The fiscal irresponsibility of Americans is only part of the problem. Retirees today began to accumulate nest eggs during postwar growth years, but now corporate cutbacks have slowed pay hikes, and earnings barely keep pace with inflation. In addition, many companies have shifted all or part of their pension and healthcare responsibilities to employees. Costs of living today are much higher, causing dual-income and single-parent families to channel money into childcare and other necessities that once would have gone into savings. Workers today cannot count on high-yield, low-risk investments like CDs, real estate, and money market funds as in earlier decades. Another common critical factor is that many American families caught in the downsizing crunch have used their savings and been forced to sell their home.

Corporate Pensions

The third leg of our retirement stool, corporate pensions, is being cut off or dramatically reduced. The end of the growth era of the private pension system of the 1940s and 1950s will only accelerate. Employers have cut their contributions 50 percent between 1980 and 1991, and private pensions now cover only 50 percent of the retired labor force. Thirty-eight percent of workers who change jobs and can take their pension money do so.

A Social Need for Raising the Retirement Age

There is another critical reason for raising the retirement age and keeping older workers in the workplace: it is a major requirement for solving the oncoming crisis of our rapidly shrinking labor force. The downsizing of the 1980s and 1990s has obscured the fact that the challenge facing U.S. companies in the twenty-first century will be to cope with an increasingly short supply of skilled knowledge workers. Our government and individual companies must now begin to consider how they can most advantageously tap and retrain this pool of older talent. The decision to extend working years will make a major difference in the size of the labor force and is a critical part of spurring the nation's rate of economic growth.

"The implications of a slower workforce are potentially ominous," according to the Hudson Institute report for 2020 (Judy and D'Amiro, 1997, p. 101). Even a slight decrease in the work-force's growth rate would mean slower economic growth just when it is most needed for the baby boomers to exit the work-force after 2010. However, workers from fifty-five to seventy years staying in the workforce would result in a more robust annual labor force growth of 1.3 percent from 1996 to 2020. That rate of increase would boost the nation's 2020 workforce by as many as 11.5 million workers, or nearly 7 percent, about the level that the nation's current trend would yield.

Summary

Study after study warns that with the scaling back of pensions, combined with the uncertain future of social security and baby boomers' poor saving habits—not to mention the high costs of housing, health care, and college—raising the retirement age is essential. Millions must rethink their financial situation, since employers and the government cannot be counted on to cover the eighteen to twenty-five years spent in retirement. Retirement planning, once considered an extra, is essential today.

The financial outlook for our generation and those that will follow is grim unless we start rethinking retirement and plan-ning realistically today. The good news is we will have the health to do so, and though we may well be forced to cut back in our lifestyle, we will go forward on a journey of personal fulfill-ment—a journey that will last until the end of our life.

CHAPTER SEVEN

Cultivating Wisdom

**To know how to grow old is the master work of wisdom and one
of the most difficult chapters in the great art of living.**

—Henri Frédéric Amiel

"Thou should'st not have been old till thou hadst been wise," the
Fool forewarned King Lear, the Shakespearean noble (act 1,
scene 5). Can we, and will we, choose to cultivate our wisdom as
we age? Some insight into this trait could prove useful for us as
we maneuver through our new century, searching for a new way
to age and add meaning to our life and our work.

Psychiatrist James Gorden, M.D., a professor at Georgetown
University School of Medicine, thinks that people should be
more concerned with wisdom and less concerned about cognition. He recommends spending some time meditating, dancing,
or performing tai chi every day, since these activities will work
on our brain chemistry too. "With an ever-increasing number of

anti-aging drugs, nutrients and hormones available and new insights into the impact lifestyles have on the brain, we may all have a lot more time to think. However, it will be up to us to grow wise" (cited in Greider, 1996, p. 70).

While we share many capabilities with other organisms, wisdom is one of the distinguishing features of humans. We are *homo sapiens,* "man, the wise." "Rather than live from moment to moment with minimal reflection and even less foresight, human beings can acquire a broad perspective on life, discerning a larger view of life's meaning than permitted by a hand to mouth subsistence" (Simonton, 1990, p. 320). This is wisdom. Such wisdom allows us to reach an equilibrium with ourselves, others, and the world, which smoothes over the vicissitudes of mundane existence.

Defining Wisdom

Wisdom, an Old English word, appeared before the year 1000, with roots in the Teutonic languages. It is defined in the *Oxford English Dictionary* (1989) as "having or exercising sound judgment or discernment; capable of judging truly concerning what is right or fitting, and disposed to act accordingly; having the ability to perceive and adopt the best means for accomplishing an end; characterized by good sense and prudence."

Wisdom encompasses the meanings of all its synonyms, suggesting a rare combination of discretion, maturity, keenness of intellect, broad experience, extensive learning, profound thought, and compassionate understanding. In its full application, wisdom implies the highest and noblest exercise of all the faculties of the moral nature as well as of the intellect. Historically, wisdom is personified almost always as female and divine. Birren and Fisher describe wisdom as being "linked with knowledge, enlightenment, learning, philosophy and science. Wisdom gives rise to wise habits and modes of action" (cited in Sternberg, 1990, p. 318).

Baltes and Smith (1990) liken wisdom to a software achievement that culture uses to outwit biological limits. They also discuss research findings in which two factors are related to wisdom. The first is an exceptional understanding, defined by common sense, learning from experience, seeing the larger context, understanding of self, open-mindedness, ability to think for oneself, and ability to see the essence of a situation. The second factor includes judgment and communication skills such as awareness, being a source of good advice, comprehending and understanding life, being worth listening to, considering all options, thinking carefully before deciding, and seeing and considering all points of view.

One current and comprehensive study of aging and wisdom, *Wisdom: Its Nature, Origins, and Development,* edited by Richard Sternberg (1990), contains chapters by different authors, each looking at complex characteristics of wisdom from different perspectives. For some it is a cognitive trait of proficiency at high-level problem solving. For others, wisdom is a complex trait contributed to by a changing balance in affective and motivational elements.

Wisdom Is in What You Are, Not in What You Do

Wisdom is more than experience. It can't be taught, measured, or weighed, and it takes decades and thousands of hours of practice to acquire. Wisdom is an expertise acquired only by growing into it. Chopra (1993) sees wisdom as a hidden bond that unites youth and old age. Frequently in the middle years our ideals are compromised to achieve success and security, with little time for the reflection necessary for wisdom. "The young are still impetuously idealistic, but the old can balance and enhance that through wisdom, perhaps the greatest gift of the human life cycle in its mature years" (p. 249).

Generally, wise persons are those who can project the consequences of their actions into the future. It's an attitude of, "I will plant trees that I will never sit under." The most wise decision is presumably what is good for the greatest number of people in the long term. Lady Bird Johnson, at age eighty-five, celebrated the founding of the National Wildflower Research Center to help us all recognize the "treasures we have in our own land" (Hoppe, 1997, p. 15). This was her wise investment in the future. "This is a scene of work, joy and friends."

In their last book, Erik Erikson (who was then in his nineties) and his wife, Joan (Erikson, Erikson, and Kivnick, 1986), defined wisdom as a detached concern with life itself and the accepting of one's life cycle as meaningful, even in the face of death. They saw wisdom as maintaining and learning to convey integrity of experience, in spite of decline of bodily and mental functions. And they warned that in an age of increasing longevity and an unpredictable technological future, wisdom will be strongly needed.

Sarason (1977) notes: "One aspect of aging is the attainment of wisdom through a process of personal experience and growth and far from fearing aging because it brings us closer to the end, we should embrace it for the truths it can reveal and the serenity which is a consequence of wisdom (p. 259)." Such a view guides the lives of too few people today.

Research on Wisdom

Surprisingly, a review of psychological material shows neglect of the concept of wisdom. The 1996 edition of the *Handbook of the*

Psychology of Aging (Birren and Schaie, 1996), with a total of 416 double-columned pages, devotes only one paragraph to wisdom, calling it an ancient topic that traditionally includes formal knowledge, moral behavior, and awareness of what one does not know. The earlier 1990 edition has one article. Another massive handbook on general psychology edited by Wolman (1973) does not index the subject, and has no mention of wisdom in its forty-five chapters.

Quite frankly, in our contemporary culture there has been a noticeable dearth of material integrating aging and wisdom in the traditional research. As a society, we are deeply uncertain and unthinking on what it means to grow old, and certainly what it means to be wise, though it is generally considered a highly valuable characteristic.

Little research and writing have been focused on aging and wisdom, yet wisdom is considered the one characteristic aging people are supposed to have in abundance. Perhaps this silence indicates a reluctance to attribute to older adults any strong positive characteristics. Birren and Fisher (cited in Sternberg, 1990) commented that "the long neglect by psychologists of the subject matter of wisdom is a curious fact that itself warrants attention" (p. 317). One reason for the neglect of wisdom in psychology could be its association with the subject of philosophy, which late-nineteenth- and early-twentieth-century psychologists placed off-limits, since they were empirically oriented behaviorists and abhorred the "mentalistic" connotation inherent in the study of wisdom.

Few researchers have attempted to look systematically at the psychology of wisdom before Paul B. Baltes (cited in White, 1993). As the director of Berlin's Max Planck Institute of Human Development and Education, he has been comparing the performance of younger and older adults on tasks involving wisdom for over a dozen years. He stresses that the "fluid mechanics" of the brain, dominated by biological conditions, may decline with age. But wisdom, where the power of human agency and culture comes into play, can improve with time.

On tests that measure a person's ability to manage the "peaks and valleys of life" and insights into the "quintessential aspects of the human condition," older adults often outperform those younger. In fact, Baltes' research found that older adults rank at the top, along with professionals who are considered wise, including clinical psychologists and experts trained to advise others about life's meaning and conduct.

Baltes also found that older adults also reflect well on difficult dilemmas of life, such as how to respond to a suicidal phone call from a friend. And they came up with good advice for a fifteen-year-old girl who wanted to get married immediately. They generated options, strategic knowledge (how to get more information, cost-benefit analysis, etc.), knowledge about the contexts of life and societal change (the individual's stage of life), and relative values and goals, and considered the uncertainties of life.

Wisdom and the Workforce

The need for wisdom is clearly demonstrated by key leaders who are moving their organizations to the twenty-first century. The editors of the *Harvard Business Review* ("Looking Ahead," 1997) asked five powerful thinkers and observers of our business world to write about the problems and challenges they see already taking shape and moving us into the future.

The five were Peter Drucker, an octogenarian who has not retired and who for decades has had the keenest foresight into the science of management and the human condition; Esther Dyson, an insightful technology analyst and entrepreneur, publisher of the newsletter *Release 1.0* and the book *Release 2.0: A Design for Living in the Digital Age* (1997); Charles Handy, oil executive, writer, and social philosopher who says he struggles to reconcile the ideals of Christian humanism with the dirty practical stuff with which business men and women have to deal; Paul Saffo, director of the Institute for the Future in California; and Peter Senge, a pioneer in organizational learning at MIT.

Interestingly enough, the resulting list of challenges from these five leaders did not include the traditional technical or rational issues; rather, it concentrated on cultural and philosophical ones, stressing the need for wisdom. The challenges were to:

- Lead organizations that create and nurture knowledge
- Know when to set machines aside and rely on our human instinct and judgment
- Live in a world where companies have increasing visibility
- Maintain, as individuals and organizations, our ability to learn
- Meet the continuing challenge—not of technology, but the art of human and humane management

Those were the five major challenges to the business world for success currently and in the future. Peter Senge (1997) discusses the implications: "Our responses may lead us, ironically, to a future based on more ancient—and more natural—ways of organizing communities of diverse and effective leaders who empower their organizations to learn with head, heart, and hand" (p. 32). This is a return to an older model of community, he says, where traditional societies that gave equal respect to elders for their wisdom, to teachers for their ability to help people grow, and to warriors, weavers, and growers for their life skills. Our new world of technology requires an abundance of, and proficiency in, wisdom, human relations skills, and sound judgment.

Mary O'Hara-Devereaux and Robert Johansen conclude their book *Global Work* (1994) with a strong statement on the

necessity of wisdom in our world today. They learned in researching and writing their book that the key to successful global enterprise was a world in which wisdom will be the coin of the global
realm and a new sense of community will be the ultimate product
of global work. This notion of wisdom as wealth and power has
been around since Plato's Socratic dialogues but has been over-
shadowed in modern times by the notion of wealth of a more
tangible source—personal consumption and possession.

Spiritual Issues Uniting Aging and Working

During the long period between the Reformation and World
War I, secular, scientific, and individualistic tendencies steadily
eroded ancient and medieval understandings of things. Old age
was removed from its ambiguous yet revered place in life's spiritual journey, rationalized, and redefined as a scientific problem
to be solved.

Our culture hasn't been interested in why or how or what it
means to grow old. Aging has been seen as an engineering problem to be solved, to be brought under the dominion of scientific
management, which is more interested in how we age, in order
to control and explain it, rather than in how to live life well.
Hence any issues involving old age become an object of social
policy: unemployment, poverty, disease, health care, retirement,
and pensions. Cole (1992) sees the problems of old age as part of
the cultural and symbolic impoverishment besetting the last half
of life since the late nineteenth century. Even the professionals
in gerontology traditionally dissociate ideas, images, and attitudes from the "facts" of aging. This dissociation of spirit from
aging makes aging an abstraction and provides a comfortable
emotional distance, making it easier to ignore. "We humans are

spiritual animals, who need love and meaning no less than food, clothing, shelter or healthcare" (p. xxi). Yet historians of aging have been slow to appreciate religion and spirituality as fundamental aspects of life. Feelings, ideas, and beliefs about aging have been judged as subjective or emotional responses to an objective reality, which impedes a rewarding understanding of growing old, both in past and present.

All societies set up systems of meaning to help people deal with limits of human existence. While religion was the dominant source in the past, science and medicine dominate them today, though this is rapidly changing as we move into the twenty-first century. There is little doubt that we are moving toward a spiritual life that integrates ancient wisdom and modern science. This integration involves combining *mystery,* which includes the cultural beliefs, values, and meanings that help us understand, accept, and imaginatively transfer the unmanageable, ambiguous aspects of existence, and *mastery,* which is dominated by the spirit/body connection and requires a definable puzzle to solve.

Jimmy Carter (cited in Hadnot, 1997) says that there is a deep stirring in this country for something that never changes, never ends—a searching for deeper truths. So much of the trust of the American people in government, the workplace, and other institutions has been abused. There is much disillusionment, and we need to look elsewhere for inspiration, truth, and guidance.

In order to eliminate age discrimination and generate positive images of aging, we need to confront the demeaning of aging that is rooted in our modern culture's relentless hostility toward the aging process. Cole (1992, p. xxviii) says that "in the late twentieth century, later life floats in a cultural limbo. It has no spiritual language." The past won't provide solutions or answers, but does provide "fundamental human stacks of ideas, feelings, images, beliefs, wishes, superstitions, dreams, hopes and fears about aging."

We must find and foster our future image for a fulfilling career with personal meaning and purpose that will provide a sense of mission and commitment. Our future image springs from and migrates through our soul, which is not synonymous with religion, but broader and deeper. It embraces the whole of us, our positive best self, and our negative or shadow self, since the human psyche has no spare parts. It's our highest sensitivity and a focus on the smallest everyday activities of life. It thrives in the mundane.

Ask yourself what feeds this part of the soul. It is what lifts our spirits. It is the highs that stay with us and reinforce us and give us strong pleasure. It can be traveling to new places and meeting people and recalling it all in your mind's eye years later. It can be growing a garden, picking the vegetables or flowers, maintaining a genuine friendship, planting a tree and watching it grow taller each year.

Conclusion

The point of successful aging and growing in wisdom is to live longer and healthier, but not necessarily staying as we were when young. Our expected increased longevity of twenty plus years simply gives us a longer time to age, learn, and grow, a time when our spirit and inner life can evolve. This means neither imitation of our youth nor decline and decay. There are special human qualities and abilities that can only come to life as we age. We can grow in maturity, understanding, acceptance, leadership, sense of humor, and giving back to society—so the movement of aging is ascending, not descending.

Ruth and Coleman (1996) say that as we grow older we should be living a *coherent* life, one that involves having an identity, a story to tell. We should strive not to see ourselves as trapped, hurt, wounded victims, but to move and shift from that story to the present time, to a perspective on self and life that involves the *eternal now*—a transcendental acceptance of self and the world. Those who arrive at retirement with conflicting internal and external identity pressures suffer the most ill effects. Though there is no guarantee that individuals, unlike King Lear, will make the right choices at those points in the life span development, those who do may be said to have grown in wisdom with age.

Resetting the Career Clock

Don't accept and act out the stereotype of being old, regardless of your chronological age. This is the first and most critical mandate for resetting the career clock in the second half of your life, the subject of Part Three. Shake off the earlier learned beliefs and misinformation about how you are supposed to act, feel, and age. Become a Ulyssean adult—a creative, curious, active learner. Forget chronology and focus on your functional age; rethink traditional retirement plans and discover and activate your vocation, calling, or mission. Cultivate wisdom, power, and purpose. If you are doing these things now, continue; if not, begin!

Knowing what you want and doing what you love is the formula for an extended life. If you are between fifty and seventy-four years of age, the age set to be the average range for the bulk of America's population in 2005, you, like many, may be well into your second midlife and wisely preparing for your capstone career. You may be searching for insight and a new kind of guidance for this next step. Many will end their first career and head into another. Drucker (1995) says the main question from women and men returning to his classes today is: "What do I need to learn so that I can decide where to go next?" Asking this learning question is the basis of moving forward. It is not, "How can I get promoted?"—the mantra of the 1970s and 1980s.

You probably dislike being stereotyped, so don't do it to yourself. You want a career that provides you with an identity that gives you meaning, money, a measure of creativity and control. You do not want the minimum wage, leftover, substitute high school teenage jobs now available for many seniors. Ideally, by this time you will have learned much from experience, worked through countless internal and external issues, and gained insight into yourself and the outside world, and you now want to put all the pieces together in a pattern to move toward a capstone career. Ideally you know what you want and will do what you love, and have initiated a career contingency action plan throughout your earlier career to achieve this capstone career, and are now ready to move forward.

Unfortunately, however, all is not ideal. Many adults have experienced debilitating and stressful career shock because of the unexpected loss of certainty and the transitional nature of work as we plunge into the Digital Age. Most adults at midlife will want meaningful and financially rewarding work but have little idea how to get it.

Many will accept the "out of the game" stereotype and severely limit themselves. Like many, you may never have sat down and consciously thought through and actually planned your career. Your approach was to work hard at your job; you considered yourself fortunate if you found it satisfying, but mainly you simply did it. Maybe you have had lots of fleeting fantasies but never considered that you could do anything even remotely connected with them. Career planning—taking responsibility for knowing yourself and what is happening in the work world so you can find the right path—is not a familiar approach. Let me assure you that this process can be learned, but it isn't quick or automatic. It requires a learning curve—active, sharp, and exciting, and frequently frustrating, like all learning curves.

Maybe you want to leave the familiar and launch out into unknown territory, trying a whole new career. Or maybe your first career is great and you want to continue, but simply refocus. Perhaps your first career was mediocre, or worse, a treadmill going nowhere—familiar, dull, but comfortable. Perhaps it was a job that you never enjoyed, but it paid the bills. Regardless, it is time to drop the negative baggage about aging and the traces of low self-esteem based on burnout or a previous career mismatch. This is no easy, quick task, but it is a necessary one in order for you to be ready to begin your search for knowing what you want to do.

CHAPTER EIGHT

Seven Steps for Resetting Your Career Clock

Where the needs of the world and your talents cross, there lies your vocation.

—Aristotle

Long before the first career winds down and you want to start another, it is critical to look at yourself and your situation carefully. This is no time for a quick survey or a "test" as your sole decision-making tool. If you are burned out, carrying a deep, dull feeling of low self-esteem—perhaps because you don't believe you have accomplished anything you particularly value in your first career or you have received no positive rewards for your work—it is critical that you spend time getting revitalized. You need to become creatively alive before you can make any additional career moves. It is essential to spend the time examining and understanding why you went into the first career. If you totally disregard this and run away and slam the door, you will react without thought or purpose. You may be vulnerable to leaving behind an important part that you will miss in your next career. Careful self-assessment and planning are an essential part of resetting your career clock.

Step 1: Recognizing Who You Are and What You Want

The first step is to discover what provides meaning and purpose for you. The discontent at midlife in our work may be because in meeting our realities and those of our cultural system we have left something important behind us. Perhaps what was left behind is a latent need or talent, existing only as potential for which there was never time or opportunity to surface and be identified. It could be that we are, at midlife or later, in the process of owning and developing a new part of ourselves.

Jung (1933) talks about the two halves of our life and the transformation at midlife. What is satisfying in the morning of our life may not be pleasing in the afternoon. Jung says that frequently at midlife, "intelligent and cultivated people have these leanings without even knowing of the possibilities of such transformations, so wholly unprepared they embark upon the second half of life" (p. 109). He points out that there are no colleges teaching or helping us to grow and develop at our midlife as there are for young people who are growing up. So "thoroughly unprepared we take the step into the afternoon of life; worse still, we take this step with the false presupposition that our truths and ideals will serve us as hitherto" (p. 108). Jung says that although the young are not to be so occupied with self, it is "the duty and necessity" for the aging person to reflect and give serious attention to her or his thoughts. Unfortunately, many at midlife have assumed the opposite, that it is futile or immature to reflect or rethink.

My clients in career unrest have verified a seemingly innate need for life balance. Often men, especially as defined in our culture, spend the first half of life triumphing over nature—competing, dominating, controlling. Wonder, creativity, compassion, and emotion are supposedly not in their realm. At midlife they may tire of ascent or, as one client put it, "stepping over dead bodies." They may begin to discover emotions, empathy and sympathy, feelings that may begin to loosen the ego. They may open their eyes to a new way to see and experience the world, and begin to grow and change. Women, on the other hand, may feel they have played out the supportive, nurturing role, and they become more competitive and venturesome. They want to sharpen their mind, perhaps moving into the workplace to test themselves. For example, my father, busy supporting eight children, had limited communication with us while we were growing up, and seemed to leave the details in the capable hands of my mother. However, when older, he declared his main role to be teaching his grandchildren how to behave properly. By this time, my mother had established a thriving business, which she ran until the age of eighty.

Let me give another example: John was a client who made a radical career change in the afternoon of his life. Earlier he had earned an MBA from Harvard. He had reached the prestigious position of CFO in two large corporations, earning well over a six-figure annual income, only to be "outplaced"—fired—from both. At no time was there any question of his ability to perform a first-rate job, but he simply didn't fit the image. One traditional outplacement firm advised him that he should stay in business management—after all, it matched his prestigious degree and experience, and besides, that's where the top money was. John, following this advice, obtained another high-level position in a bank, but within a short time was out of a job again.

I remember vividly the first time I met John. I saw a Volkswagen drive up, and getting out was a rather casual-looking, slow-moving man of about fifty-five. With hair that turned up at his shirt collar and wearing a tweed coat, loose khaki pants, argyle socks, and loafers, he reminded me of my college English professors. Was this the former CFO to some of the largest banking institutions in the country?

John's car and his appearance were the first strong clues that he was different from the investment bankers he had interacted with daily. This client turned out to have a brilliant mind—but absolutely no interest in the practical application of business. His warrior skills were nonexistent. He, based on all our interviews and assessments, was the philosopher, the thinker—the most academic and investigative client I've encountered.

Some assessments showed him to have the perfect career profile for a college philosophy or psychology professor, with the highest possible aptitude for research and writing. His interest in and comfort with college environments were extremely high, much higher than would be indicated by the average happily working, enterprising MBA. Every trait on John's personality profile and interest inventory showed directly opposite that of the traditional business executive. This was also strongly affirmed by his many outside interests; for example, he had been taking psychology courses in his free time for three semesters.

John admitted that he had never felt like he belonged in the financial world. Now, at midlife, he simply couldn't maintain the mask any longer. A brilliant man miscast, his interests were philosophy, psychology, art, literature, mathematics, and concepts. When asked why he had gone to business school, he explained he had seen Humphrey Bogart, the cool, detached, sophisticated businessman in *Sabrina Fair*, and based on that image decided to go to business school—totally a mismatch for him.

This was a real loss to society, since he would have been a brilliant research psychologist, mathematician, or writer. The cause of the career problems surfaced at once—but not a creative solution. As a result of much insight, soul-searching, and research, John made the decision to become a math and computer science teacher in an exclusive private school. He is an excellent teacher, enjoys his work, and has no regrets about leaving the world of business or giving up his corporate salary.

At this time, many professional career women, without giving it real thought, have been willing to be in a career that has limited meaning for them—since they expected to marry and have children, which would provide the *real* meaning. Sometime in their forties—often unmarried—many realize that they can't count on this. This realization, coupled with limited career satisfaction, leads to an active search for more meaningful work.

One lawyer in her early forties told me: "What will be my mark in the world? My work in law is OK; I can do it. It's not bad, but it makes no real difference that is uniquely me." After being strongly encouraged to explore what held a natural interest for her outside of work, she is discovering that she has a real gift for writing children's stories. As she says, "They just come to me. I instinctively know how children feel and what they need to know."

Interestingly enough, while she, like many attorneys, has a high artistic need coupled with a social helping/teaching need, evident from all her assessments and our conversations, her direct interaction with children in groups or on a one-to-one basis is limited. She expresses her caring and concern through stories that spring from her own childhood. Her creativity and the confidence to express these stories emerged only after she relaxed her need for approval by constantly pushing through to a status law career.

She has decided to stay in law to pay her bills and will do an excellent job, but her "mark" and meaning will come from writing for children, and her natural intensity has moved to that focus. An important part of resetting the career clock involves going back to get reacquainted with who you were when you were very young—to trace yourself and your aspirations and move them to the present, though perhaps in a different form.

Deciding what will bring you real satisfaction in your work and which option has the most promise can be a real challenge, since introspection has not been encouraged, especially in men. As one male client, a very successful sales representative for medical equipment, put it: "This self-assessment is the most difficult—my greatest challenge. You don't realize how little experience I've had doing this in my life." A great number of women have had limited work experience to use as a judgment base. Many at midlife have focused on what they had to do, or on what they perceived they were "supposed" to do, and have not spent quality, focused time in assessing what is really important.

To move successfully into your capstone career, at midlife— or second midlife—it is essential that you reassess what is important to you. Frequently, I have noted that those who have a myopic image built on rigid external views of themselves can begin to feel professionally successful when they drop this false persona, discover what they are really all about, and accept who they are with their own special and individualized mystique, including flaws, strengths, eccentricities, and foibles. They will also begin to meet people who are attracted to them as they really are—the genuine, authentic person long hidden behind the external mask.

On the following pages are several exercises designed to help you rethink your future direction.

EXERCISE 1   *Life Cycle Chart*

1. On the following page, depict a chronological history of key events, transitions, or crises of your personal and professional life. You may use a simple line, a curving upward spiral, a hill and valley profile, or any other method. I frequently learn as much about people by how they approach this as by what they write.

2. After you complete your Life Line, go back over the key events and rate each with a plus or minus, depending on how you feel it affected your life.

3. Answer the following questions:

What do the key events in your life have in common?

How lengthy are the plateaus between these key events?

Is there any pattern in the way you dealt with crises or solved problems?

When did you make your best decisions? Why?

Which events were true crises in your life? What triggered them?

What were your peak experiences? What made them peaks?

What risks did you take?

If you generalized about the kind of life you have had, would it be flat, up and down, exciting, boring, risky, volatile, or what?

What have you learned about yourself from drawing this chart and examining it?

EXERCISE 1   *Life Cycle Chart (cont'd)*

Key Events Life Line

Personal Development Life Line

Career Life Line

EXERCISE 2   *Assessing Personal Needs*

Assess your personal needs at the present time. In the empty block following each numbered item, assign a point value to it, using the values below. Then add each column and transfer the score to page 137 by placing an X on your score for each column.

15—"I always feel an obsessive need to..."   **5—"I feel an occasional need to..."**
10—"I feel a frequent need to..."   **0—"I seldom or never feel a need to..."**

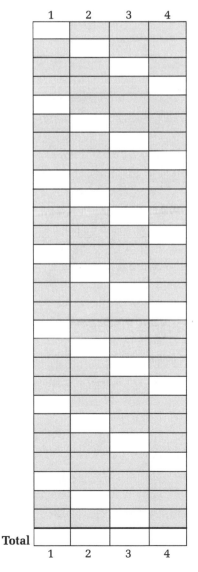

	1	2	3	4
1. Pursue perfection and excellence.				
2. Avoid unpleasant jobs.				
3. Help others.				
4. Spend time alone.				
5. Attempt to do things better.				
6. Avoid involved tasks.				
7. Be trusted by friends.				
8. Do something for myself rather than for another.				
9. Stay with a task until it is finished.				
10. Have more time for leisure activities.				
11. Offer affection toward others.				
12. Keep people at arm's length.				
13. Accomplish something noteworthy.				
14. Put things off until later.				
15. Make others feel good.				
16. Deal with things rather than people.				
17. Tackle a tough task.				
18. Avoid getting involved.				
19. Work with a group instead of alone.				
20. Avoid the "rat race."				
21. Be productive.				
22. Maintain the status quo.				
23. Go along with decisions of others.				
24. Work alone.				
25. Be a winner.				
26. Be entertained when not busy (TV, games, etc.).				
27. Get suggestions and aid from others.				
Total				
	1	2	3	4

EXERCISE 2 *Assessing Personal Needs (cont'd)*

15—"I always feel an obsessive need to..."   5—"I feel an occasional need to..."
10—"I feel a frequent need to..."   0—"I seldom or never feel a need to..."

	5	6	7	8
28. Avoid small talk as a waste of time.				
29. Have others do it my way.				
30. Do what others suggest.				
31. Have others think well of me.				
32. Break out with something new.				
33. Criticize others.				
34. Have someone else lead.				
35. Follow others' opinions.				
36. Do my own thing.				
37. Take charge of things.				
38. Avoid doing things on my own initiative.				
39. Wait for new styles to be accepted before trying.				
40. Do the right thing despite the consequences.				
41. Have influence or charm others.				
42. Follow set habits and tradition.				
43. Avoid decision making.				
44. Stand out from others.				
45. Settle disputes.				
46. Gain opinions of others before deciding.				
47. Discuss my viewpoints and past successes.				
48. Voice different ideas and opinions than others.				
49. Use books, ideas, etc., to influence and persuade.				
50. Obey figures of authority (police, boss, etc.).				
51. Receive others' attention.				
52. Act without interference.				
53. Make decisions for the group.				
54. Be talked out of things by others.				
55. Obtain encouragement and support from others.				
56. Be the center of attention.				
Total				
	5	6	7	8

E X E R C I S E   2   *Assessing Personal Needs (cont'd)*

Personal Needs Assessment

	10	15	20	25	30	35	40	45	50	55	60	65	70	75	80	85	90	95	100
1. Achievement																			
2. Contentment																			
3. Belonging																			
4. Isolation																			
5. Dominance																			
6. Deference																			
7. Acceptance																			
8. Individualism																			

Achievement	Test self against others and own earlier accomplishments, perform well at increasingly challenging, demanding tasks.
Contentment	Relax and enjoy leisure by avoiding arduous demands and pressure; satisfaction with what one has or is.
Belonging	To interact, communicate, and feel accepted by others; have close friends, be extroverted, like variety and action.
Isolation	Work alone without interference or consultation with others—introverted; deal internally with ideas.
Dominance	Control others, make decisions, influence events, gain acceptance for one's views and opinions, be the leader and take charge.
Deference	Follow another's lead, seek advice and encouragement, and avoid acting on one's own initiative; good follower.
Acceptance	Gain approval and acceptance of a supportive manager and the group and have its support; be on a team, work with others.
Individualism	Stand out or be different, act on one's own judgment, and resist social pressure: do it your way, dislike micro-management!

These needs are opposites, and we usually have some of each. Check your higher score from each pair. Close scores on a pair, **within 10 points,** illustrate the potential for conflict unless you are aware of the pull in opposing directions and make the necessary adjustments. In other words, there is no automatic pilot or cruise control when dealing with these opposing needs. Decisions may need to be consciously made. Your awareness is the key.

E X E R C I S E 3   *Major Accomplishments*

Make a vivid but brief story of your accomplishments. Religious teachers speak in parables because people remember these. Review your work history and list your strengths: now select an accomplishment that demonstrates this strength in action. Tell a story!

1. Skill: _____ Accomplishment: _____

    Where? Setting/place: _____ Others involved or alone: _____

    What? Problem/conflict faced: _____

    _____

    How? Actions you took: _____

    _____

    _____

    Results for others/company: _____

    Payoff for you: _____

2. Skill: _____ Accomplishment: _____

    Where? Setting/place: _____ Others involved or alone: _____

    What? Problem/conflict faced: _____

    _____

    How? Actions you took: _____

    _____

    _____

    Results for others/company: _____

    Payoff for you: _____

3. Skill: _____ Accomplishment: _____

    Where? Setting/place: _____ Others involved or alone: _____

    What? Problem/conflict faced: _____

    _____

    How? Actions you took: _____

    _____

    _____

    Results for others/company: _____

    Payoff for you: _____

Step 2: Developing Your Success Criteria List

Deciding what are your "glass balls," that is, the elements that are so critical for us to feel successful that we cannot drop them—as opposed to our "rubber balls" those issues that can be dropped without great loss—is critical. Writing out your success criteria list—your glass balls—will help you move forward with purpose and direction.

Many younger parents decide that paying close attention to rearing their children is a glass ball—we don't get a second chance at this. Maintaining one's health, whatever that takes, is certainly a glass ball. My clients also list other ones: staying on a learning curve, defined as staying on the cutting edge of gaining new information and understanding; independence, control, meaning, autonomy, and making their own decisions without interference; creativity, defined as expressing themselves; job location; and maintaining a high level of integrity in their work. Your success criteria reflect your value system. Completing Exercise 4 on pages 140–141, " Values Inventory," could be helpful in your thinking. But make sure you add to it.

As you go through the process of determining your values, you will bring to the surface factors that are deeply important. These "glass balls" become your *success criteria*—what you must have to feel successful about yourself and your work life. These criteria spring from your core values and are as unique as your fingerprints. They are your individualized bedrock, your prescription, your map for what to do next. They are *not* what society or someone else tells you that you should want. If you know and maintain your success criteria, you can cut through the stress and chaos of our changing and shifting work world. Without this, you cannot be in control of your work life, and believe me, if you aren't in charge, no one is. Some clients, especially males, will quickly tell me initially that making a six-figure income is their first and major success criterion. Frequently this

EXERCISE 4   *Values Inventory*

Below are seventy values—select your top-ten *always valued*. Then rank and write them in order of importance to you. Write those you *never valued* and want to avoid. On a scale of 1 to 10 (10 = highest), rate the amount of each value you have now in your life and work. You may use any number each number of times.

Absorbing work	_____	Requires thought/activity on evenings/weekends
Advancement	_____	Work hard and advance rapidly
Adventure	_____	Have duties that involve frequent risk taking
Aesthetics	_____	Be involved in study or appreciation of beauty
Autonomy	_____	Set own goals and work without close supervision
Balance	_____	Integrate needs of personal life—family, friends, self
Casual dress	_____	Wear casual, comfortable clothing to work
Challenge	_____	Solve difficult problems and avoid routine
Change & variety	_____	Have duties that change frequently
Commitment	_____	Feel pride in product or service
Community	_____	Be involved in community affairs
Compatibility	_____	Work with people who share same interests and values
Compensation	_____	Good salary and other financial rewards
Competence	_____	Work where I have talents above the average
Competition	_____	Pit my abilities against those of others
Corporate culture	_____	Integrity of organization merits my loyalty
Creativity	_____	Create original ideas, programs, or products
Education benefits	_____	Continue my education through job benefits
Enthusiasm	_____	Work with people who are energized and challenged
Environment	_____	Work in pleasant and comfortable surroundings
Ethics	_____	Perform work consistent with strong personal beliefs
Excellence	_____	Product is recognized as outstanding
Excitement	_____	Experience a high degree of exhilaration in my work
Family	_____	Keep the needs of my family a first priority
Fast pace	_____	Work at a fast pace and perform work rapidly
Feedback	_____	Gain information on performance
Fixed hours	_____	Have set hours and free time
Free agent	_____	Determine projects, time, purpose, and environment
Friendships	_____	Have close relationships with colleagues
Fringe benefits	_____	Have good medical insurance and vacation time
Generalist	_____	Use broad knowledge of many areas in work
Help others	_____	Help or serve people
Help society	_____	Work to contribute toward bettering the world
High earnings	_____	Obtain the essentials and luxuries that I want
Incentive pay	_____	Have financial rewards depend on results
Independence	_____	Determine nature of work without interference
Influence people	_____	Change attitudes and opinions of others
Innovation	_____	See work on latest cutting edge of my industry
Intellectual status	_____	Be regarded as an expert in my field
Job tranquility	_____	Avoid extreme pressure and the "rat race"
Knowledge	_____	Pursue truth, knowledge, and human understanding
Leisure	_____	Devote energy to personal and leisure activities
Location	_____	Work in a particular geographic area

EXERCISE 4   *Values Inventory (cont'd)*

Make decisions	_____	Decide policy or course of action
Management	_____	Be responsible for work of others to produce results
Mentor	_____	Work under someone whose guidance I respect
Moral fulfillment	_____	Work to further important moral standards
Personal development	_____	Workplace encourages self-growth
Physical challenge	_____	Be rewarded for superior physical ability
Policies & practices	_____	Company treats its employees fairly
Power & authority	_____	Control the actions and lives of others
Precision	_____	Work at an exacting job
Predictability	_____	Have a well-ordered workday with few surprises
Pressure	_____	Work under deadlines and critical judgment
Professional growth	_____	Learn new ideas or skills at work
Profit, Gain	_____	Accumulate money or material rewards
Public contact	_____	Maintain day-to-day contacts with people
Recognition	_____	Achieve visible and public recognition
Reputation	_____	Work for a well-known and respected organization
Security	_____	Be assured of keeping job and having a steady income
Self-expression	_____	Be able to convey my ideas to improve my job
Service	_____	Feel work benefits others
Spirit	_____	Opportunity to be full of spirit, animated, and lively
Spiritual	_____	Work activities connect inner values to outside realities
Stability	_____	Have predictable and regular work routine
Staff position	_____	Work in a support or advisory function
Status	_____	Gain respect from friends, family, and community
Strategic thinking	_____	Involvement in innovative and visionary thinking
Structure	_____	Receive clear direction as to goals and procedures
Submissiveness	_____	Need to follow another's lead, seek advice and encouragement, avoid acting on own initiative
Supervision	_____	Be directly responsible for work of others
Teamwork	_____	Work with others to reach goals
Technical work	_____	Be an expert in a specialized field
Time freedom	_____	Set own schedule and hours
Travel	_____	Move from place to place
Visibility	_____	Do work noticeable to higher management
Work alone	_____	Have little contact with others on the job

Always Valued	Rate	Never Valued	Rate
1.			
2.			
3.			
4.			
5.			
6.			
7.			
8.			
9.			
10.			

Rate the amount you have in life/work NOW

E X E R C I S E 5 *Determining Your Success Criteria*

Thoughtfully determine and list your "glass balls"—your strongest, most fundamental career needs for your success. Then write down how you determine your measure of success in each category and rate each career option between 1 and 10 (10 is the highest).

Career Options (Rated 1–10)

My Career Success Criteria	As Measured or Quantified by				

Option Totals

EXERCISE 5 *Determining Your Success Criteria (cont'd)*

Sample

Career Options (Rated 1–10)

My Career Success Criteria	As Measured or Quantified by	Current job	Previous job	Career/job being considered	
Creativity in work	Solving problems in new ways	2	2	7	
Variety	Many different daily activities	2	4	6	
Team environment	Work with compatible people	4	1	7	
Balance	Time for family	5	3	3	

Option Totals	13	10	23	

is because our society has geared them to think of success only in terms of money and status. As they work through their self-assessment process this may move off their list entirely. Exercise 5, "Determining Your Success Criteria," will help you in your self-assessment process.

As you bring your success criteria to the surface, it helps to give a brief but specific description of how you will know when you are achieving that particular criterion. Bill's myth buster is the story of his list of success criteria and his account of how he used it to evaluate his new position—a change from being a partner in a law firm, which he saw as highly adversarial, both

Success Criteria Sheet

1. Intellectual challenge: Learning curve high, not routine.

2. Creativity: Developing a business or something useful.

3. Teamwork: Work in positive environment with nonadversarial colleagues.

4. Peer recognition: Seen as one of the best in my field.

5. Ethics: Honest people with high standards, trustworthy.

6. Contact with people: Daily interaction with others.

7. Producing something of value: Influence, leave a mark. Help create a new business or something of intrinsic value.

8. Financial rewards: Able to pay for education of my children.

9. Flexibility: Set my own schedule.

10. Aesthetics, visual and aural: Contact with the arts; use these senses.

On this, the first day of my new job, I believe that I will enjoy all but the last two items (9 and 10) in my new position. As one of the lead lawyers responsible for the sales/franchise relationships in the United States for the company, I certainly will be challenged intellectually and must work in a team-oriented environment with the businesspeople. This position involves daily contact with the businesspeople, so I will have much contact with other people, especially the franchise and sales staff. Producing a product of value is evident, especially if you like soft drinks and chocolate.

The financial rewards are also present as the benefits are great and the salary is excellent, especially when joined with stock options, bonuses, and stock purchase plan. I even get a company car!

The main thing I am giving up is flexibility on my hours, although the legal department is quite flexible, with only four lawyers. Hours are set at 8 A.M. to 5 P.M., but I expect to work more than that. I am certainly happy to give up a little flexibility in order to have a team-oriented and successful environment where I can expand my practice area and experience a high degree of ethical standards. These are very important to me. As far as visual/aural goes, I will certainly use those skills in dealing with the businesspeople daily. The aesthetics criterion is my least concern—I can just play the piano a little more on the weekends.

I will be reporting to the general counsel and will be the lead attorney in the U.S. in charge of all sales and franchise relationships. I will be communicating daily with the businesspeople on sales/franchise issues that arise, e.g., problems with underperforming bottler franchisers, and will also manage litigation and labor/employment litigation as needed. I also will be involved in corporate acquisitions as they arise. My practice area will be much broader and more business oriented—and much more team oriented. My business goals are no longer to bill hours and to originate business, but to further the business of the company.

I recommend that people talk informally with as many people they can who hold positions similar to the position sought, both for information purposes and for connecting and community purposes. I got this position from the recommendation of one of my former partners who had heard that I was seeking an in-house posi

tion. Fortunately, I had told a lawyer friend who worked with the former partner, and the former partner recommended me to the general counsel at my new company.

Patience and diligence are also key. I researched my new company thoroughly prior to each of my five interviews and dropped tidbits during my interviews showing my knowledge.

The final hint is to listen to yourself and to follow what you want to do. Clear your head, listen to your desires and goals, and, finally, talk to as many people as you can to network and research the area you wish to target.

---

within his firm and in his professional activity. He has become an in-house corporate lawyer. His undergraduate degree was in English as a major and business as a minor. Bill was promoted to chief counsel for one of his organization's major firms.

Step 3: Matching Internal Needs with External Realities

The process of finding both meaning for yourself and money for your future involves taking a hard look at reality and answering some important questions. Asking questions is an important initial step in the process of change. You need to think through what I refer to as the "grail questions" earlier in the book. These questions are designed to structure the thinking process, not to come up with final answers. Exercise 6 "Challenge of Change," includes some of the earliest grail questions I ask my clients to begin thinking through.

One client, burned out from twenty years as an interior designer, saw from her point of view a need for a really tasty chocolate cookie. She brought a family recipe successfully to the public by using her design talent for the packaging to accompany the great product. Today her business is thriving. Another client, a partner in a law firm with an undergraduate degree in business, declared that he wanted to make deals, not advise others on them. In 1995, he teamed up with a talented technologist and cofounded a company that integrated his business savvy with his entrepreneurial spirit and love of sports. Under his leadership, his company became a trailblazing pioneer in developing the Internet as a new broadcast medium. Its IPO soared to a record high in its first day of trading.

Three years earlier, all he knew about technology and computers was word processing and how to program his VCR. He jumped outside his strictly legal box, recognizing an opportunity, and quickly learned what he needed to know to build a successful operation. This is a process of moving beyond our fears and taking educated, calculated risks.

To develop your capstone career, be assertive about exploring what you might like to do; become extremely curious. If you think of a question, it is worthy of asking, so ask questions, and ask more questions. Discover and validate what interests you. Read, talk to people, visit organizations, volunteer at civic and community organizations. This may not lead you directly to a career, but it will loosen up your thinking so you can get your creative juices flowing. Many adults at midlife are frozen into tunnel vision. We must move outside the tunnel and explore.

E X E R C I S E 6   *Challenge of Change*

1. What five words would you use to describe today's change?

2. What do you see as your greatest challenge in the future?

3. What is your greatest challenge now in the present?

4. What is your greatest strength for dealing successfully with your future?

5. What is your greatest fear concerning your future? How can you reduce this fear?

6. What is your greatest fear about the present? How can you reduce this now?

7. If you were given a gift of foresight, the ability to gain answers about your future, what three questions would you ask?
   a. _____
   b. _____
   c. _____

8. Using three circles, draw a picture showing how you feel about the past, present, and future.

9. List three words that describe your current situation.

10. List three words that you see as describing your future.

I tell my clients that this is getting a doctorate in "what's happening out there."

In order to become actively aware and curious about the world outside your "box," you need to brainstorm. I have found that there are four critical grail questions that need to be asked in order to match your internal needs with the reality of the external world. These questions are listed on a worksheet in Exercise 7 "Critical Grail Questions for Creative Change." Take some time now to look at them and write down your answers or think about them.

Matching your internal and external needs is not always an easy or direct process. While millions have a strong desire to do something with more meaning and purpose, a real problem with most "successful" men and women at midlife is that they have focused and concentrated so strongly on what they perceived was "success" that they have no real idea what will give them deeper meaning and purpose beyond the money and status, and certainly no vocabulary to express it. Consciously discovering, articulating, and pursuing this goal has not been fashionable or allowable in our pragmatic culture, especially for highly educated professionals who were supposed to love their work based on the status of their profession.

We must continue to learn about ourselves, others, and the world we live in, and enjoy this learning. Einstein (1942) wrote his friend Otto Juliusberger on a trait he found critical to his successful aging. "People like you and me, though mortal, of course, like everyone else, do not grow old no matter how long we live. What I mean is that we never cease to stand like curious children before the great mystery into which we were born" (p. 238).

Adaptive skills are our personality traits that determine how we relate to our world. Acquired through both "nature" and "nurture"—springing from our DNA and learned from our environment— they are critical for a good job or career fit. Exercise 8, "Adaptive Self-Management Skills" on pages 150–151 can help you assess the effectiveness of your adaptive skills.

EXERCISE 7 *Critical Grail Questions for Creative Change*

What does the world need now or in the future?

Do I have the skills to meet that need or can I get them?

Would I value doing that and could I make a commitment to it?

Can I make a living doing these things? How?

E X E R C I S E 8 *Adaptive Self-Management Skills*

Our personality weaknesses frequently are an overextension of our strengths.
Balance is critical. Check the effective and ineffective adaptive self-management
skills that describe you.

Effective	Ineffective
❏ Original	❏ Unrealistic
❏ Imaginative	❏ "Far out"
❏ Creative	❏ Fantasy-bound
❏ Broad-gauged	❏ Scattered
❏ Charismatic	❏ Devious
❏ Idealistic	❏ Out of touch
❏ Ideological	❏ Impractical
❏ Intellectually tenacious	❏ Dogmatic
❏ Effective communicator	❏ Verbose
❏ Deliberative	❏ Indecisive
❏ Prudent	❏ Overcautious
❏ Weighs alternatives	❏ Overanalyzes
❏ Stabilizing	❏ Unemotional
❏ Objective	❏ Nondynamic
❏ Rational	❏ Controlled
❏ Analytical	❏ Overserious
❏ Spontaneous	❏ Impulsive
❏ Persuasive	❏ Manipulative
❏ Empathetic	❏ Overpersonalize
❏ Traditional values	❏ Sentimental
❏ Probing	❏ Postponing
❏ Introspective	❏ Guilt ridden
❏ Draws out feelings	❏ Stirs up conflict
❏ Loyal	❏ Subjective
❏ Pragmatic	❏ Shortsighted
❏ Assertive, directional	❏ Status seeking
❏ Results oriented	❏ Self-involved
❏ Objective	❏ Lacks trust
❏ Perfection seeking	❏ Nit-picking

E X E R C I S E   8   *Adaptive Self-Management Skills (cont'd)*

Here are some additional adjectives that could describe how you effectively adapt to your environment. Check the five that best describe you. Rank them from 1 to 5 (1 = highest) in order of intensity. Now write in each trait and what you think could be the result of carrying it too far (to the point of ineffectiveness).

- ❑ Adventurous
- ❑ Aggressive
- ❑ Ambitious
- ❑ Analytical
- ❑ Attention getting
- ❑ Calm
- ❑ Capable
- ❑ Committed
- ❑ Competent
- ❑ Complicated
- ❑ Conscientious
- ❑ Conservative
- ❑ Convincing
- ❑ Cooperative
- ❑ Creative
- ❑ Critical
- ❑ Curious
- ❑ Dependable
- ❑ Disorderly

- ❑ Domineering
- ❑ Efficient
- ❑ Energetic
- ❑ Emotional
- ❑ Empathetic
- ❑ Expressive
- ❑ Fair
- ❑ Flexible
- ❑ Frank
- ❑ Friendly
- ❑ Generous
- ❑ Helpful
- ❑ Honest
- ❑ Humble
- ❑ Idealistic
- ❑ Imaginative
- ❑ Impractical
- ❑ Impulsive
- ❑ Independent

- ❑ Inhibited
- ❑ Insightful
- ❑ Intellectual
- ❑ Introverted
- ❑ Intuitive
- ❑ Kind
- ❑ Logical
- ❑ Materialistic
- ❑ Methodical
- ❑ Modest
- ❑ Natural
- ❑ Nonconforming
- ❑ Obedient
- ❑ Optimistic
- ❑ Orderly
- ❑ Original
- ❑ Outgoing
- ❑ Persistent
- ❑ Pleasure seeking

- ❑ Popular
- ❑ Practical
- ❑ Precise
- ❑ Rational
- ❑ Reserved
- ❑ Responsible
- ❑ Self-confident
- ❑ Self-controlled
- ❑ Serious
- ❑ Shy
- ❑ Sincere
- ❑ Sociable
- ❑ Stable
- ❑ Tenacious
- ❑ Tolerant
- ❑ Trustworthy
- ❑ Understanding
- ❑ Versatile
- ❑ Wise

Select and list your top five below; think through what could be a weakness if this strength is carried too far.

My strengths = *effective*	Carried too far = *weakness or ineffectiveness*
1.	
2.	
3.	
4.	
5.	

Step 4: Exploring Career Options

After some real thought on and exploration of internal and external realities, you may find some formal career assessment tools helpful in sorting through your career options. I don't refer to these as tests, since I see them only as tools to help in decision making. They should not be used exclusively, regardless of their reliability or validity.

In working with adults, I use about a dozen such tools, depending on my assessment of their circumstances. Most of these, with the exception of the MBTI, tie in to the research of Dr. John Holland (1997) and to his theory of vocational personalities and work environments. Deceptively simple but extremely well-researched and translated into many languages, his *Self-Directed Search* is a basic tool that determines a three-letter assessment code for the taker. An Occupational Finder booklet lists likely careers for each matching three-letter code. This assessment tool ties in your past work history since it includes your skills—what you can do—even though you may not want to use these skills. Here are some assessment tools:

- The *Strong Interest Inventory*®, a valuable tool in career planning, focuses strictly on interests, not on skills or abilities. It suggests occupations compatible with your highest interests and also compares your interests to those of people working in specific occupations.

- The *16 Personality Factors*® (with a Career Profile narration developed by Dr. Vern Walters) provides a Holland code for personality traits but cautions that we should beware of selecting a career based strictly on personality traits.

- The *Myers-Briggs Type Indicator*® (MBTI®), based on Jung's theory of personalities, is extremely helpful in self-assessment and provides a list of careers that match personality type.

I hesitate to discuss vocational assessment since too many adults think that taking a career assessment alone will provide the absolute answer. I caution that we should understand what is being assessed, and use the results as indicators, not absolutes. I insist that my clients give some very real thought to their career situation before we study the results of their formal assessment. While they do gain much information, I instruct them to cross out what they see as invalid for them, since even the best assessment instruments have a margin of error. These vocational tools will provide information, but they cannot in and of themselves solve a complex career change problem for a midlife adult.

Most career counselors use these basic tools, or they can often be taken at a college career center. I also provide these on my Web site **(http://www.career-design.com)**.

Step 5: Developing a Future Focus and Direction

Mindfully integrating who we are and what we want, determining our success criteria and matching these up with viable career options, and visualizing ourselves in our future give us the direction essential to career planning.

It is especially important in career planning at midlife that we see ourselves actually doing what we have decided to do. The power of intention based on thoughtful assessment and judgment fuels and fires our purpose and personal power. Mentally picturing where we want to be programs our direction. This is where the pieces of the puzzle come together into a coherent whole. As Kitty, a talented and creative client, expressed it: "The pieces have been there jumbled up in a box all the time, but crumbled and frayed on so many sides, I just had to carefully smooth them out to see how they fit together."

E X E R C I S E   9   *Creating Your Future Job: Proposal for Innovation*

Use this as a guideline for using your ideas, skills, and experience to solve a problem.

I.   Proposal: define your proposal in one sentence

   1.   Identify background: problems and needs

   2.   Develop a solution

   3.   Demonstrate benefits

   4.   Why me?

      a. knowledge

      b. skills, talents

      c. enthusiasm

      d. related experience

II.   Cost estimate (optional)

   1.   Negotiating

      a. What would you ideally want for doing this?

      b. What are essential factors that you would not trade off?

Often you can create your future image, your direction, without leaving your present environment. When there is a problem to be solved at work and you can see an innovative solution, use the outline in Exercise 9 to design a proposal and present it to a key decision maker. This has worked for many of my clients in creating a job they can enjoy.

Step 6: Developing a Strategic Action Plan

How do I get to my future image? Reaching this goal requires a plan based on information, resourcefulness, innovation, and planned action steps to be taken over a period of time. It could include finding a new job in the same field, refocusing your current job, making a radical career change, starting a business, or perhaps becoming a full-time volunteer in a nonprofit organization you value. Whatever your choice, setting goals and acting on them systematically and creatively are absolutely essential.

Insight without action serves no purpose in resetting your career clock. While mindless activity does not serve a real purpose, neither do procrastination and delaying tactics. For many clients, gaining direction from visualizing a future picture of themselves is all they need to stimulate their action. For others, self-defeating behavior habits must be identified and discarded. Fear, anxiety, and apprehension at moving out of the known comfort zone have them in their grip. This negative reaction will often become very intense at the critical time of action, then gradually it begins to dissipate as clients see clearly what they are doing to shoot themselves in the foot! Exercise 10 will help you embark on a critical path for action results.

EXERCISE 10   *Critical Path for Action Results*

Career-Family-Financial-Mental-Physical-Spiritual-Social

My major/lifetime mission: _____

Goals for period _____ to _____

Use green ink for steps taken, write "nothing" in red ink if you took no steps.

Goal 1   **Goal 2**

To Do	Steps Taken	To Do	Steps Taken

EXERCISE 10   *Critical Path for Action Results (cont'd)*

Goal 3   **Goal 4**

To Do	Steps Taken	To Do	Steps Taken

Are your goals specific?

Are they time-framed?

Are they attainable?

Are they relevant?

Step 7: Seeing Yourself as a Pathfinder on a New Frontier

Thomas Paine, the "spark plug of the American Revolution," was born into a Quaker family in England. He worked as a tax collector, a job that fired in him a passion to eliminate social inequity. Benjamin Franklin persuaded him to emigrate to America, where he was made an editor of the *Pennsylvania Magazine.* A modern thinker, Paine demonstrated fearlessness and originality of thought, advocating ideas far ahead of his time—women's rights, freedom for slaves, a system of international arbitration, national and international copyright, and kindness to animals. He gave up his job and joined Washington's army in 1776 when it was retreating across New Jersey in bitter defeat. Sitting on a log alongside a campfire, with a drumhead for a desk, he penned the immortal words that began: "These are the times that try men's souls. . . ." Washington ordered these words read to his shivering men, words that only days later undoubtedly helped inspire the surprising defeat of the British at Trenton.

Only a few hundred years ago, a brief instant in our history, we were fighting a revolution for independence against external powers limiting our political freedom. Today we are struggling in another revolution. This one is a revolution of *change,* a soul-trying, chaotic battle where much of what is familiar is being abruptly swept away. We are struggling to regain our *internal* independence and freedom, not from a foreign invader but from our own beliefs and perceptions of what our lives "should and ought" to be, as earlier prescribed by convention and our expectations.

During the last fifty years, following the formula instituted in the Depression Era, we sought out and set up an established system to guarantee lifetime security primarily based on materialism, growing affluence, a womb-to-tomb corporate career-ladder job with automatic annual salary increases, the accumulation of advanced specialized degrees for status careers (not necessarily more insight or learning), and full insurance coverage for all possible adversities. We didn't exactly sell our soul, but we passively settled for external security and materialistic comfort. This external security, however, has not translated internally and therefore has not resulted in a sense of power, purpose, or meaning.

In today's rapidly changing world, we are realizing that our former expectations and rules are becoming meaningless. Our previous drive for an external security system has come at a high price. Many have lost the instinct for personal survival, long since traded off for long-term security from an external source. This silencing of our survival instincts has had serious repercussions. We're strangers to ourselves and what we can do. We don't see how we can live without all our former trappings, even though they carry a cavity of meaninglessness in our soul. We surrendered our personal independence, our willingness to embrace a new challenge, and our creativity. We settled for the tyranny of the formula and for maintaining an outdated, established system that has ceased to support us. We stepped on a treadmill going nowhere. We passed countless challenging opportunities, traded off self-confidence, and became passive, dependent children, with a deep-seated fear of facing adversity. And now, what we see ahead for our own children and grandchildren is dim, if not downright dark. In making decisions, the Iroquois always had a seventh-generation question—How would their present action affect the seventh generation following? But we have been woefully lacking in this type of wisdom and foresight. We fret and frustrate ourselves in our fruitless frivolities and fear.

Cynicism, bitterness, depression, anger, and anxiety constitute the way many Americans are handling their lost expectations. Addiction—to drugs, alcohol, sex, shopping, and work— is another technique for escaping our disappointments and nameless fears. We can choose to be victims without insight or options, slaves to the established system of our internal beliefs. We can keep doing the same things, expecting different results. Or we can choose to follow the advice of Mother Teresa, who said that she never thought of making a difference with forty thousand people, but saw only one person at a time. The move toward personal independence and responsibility—becoming a free agent—is a step forward. To thrive in the twenty-first century, we must cultivate the ability to see ourselves as pathfinders. We must move through our present turbulence and make choices with some grace, courage, independence, and self-reliance. As Paine said, tyranny, even that of our own making, is not easily conquered.

Today we are experiencing countless revolutions of change on almost every front. Paine said that it appears that "revolutions create genius and talents, but those events do no more than bring them forward. There is existing in man a mass of sense lying in a dormant state, and which, unless something excites it to action, will descend with him, in that condition, to the grave." Our challenge today, both to bring value to ourselves and to our society, is to unfreeze our dormant supply of genius and talent to serve the many needs of our world.

A *future image* of ourselves, a vision we value, will bring forth our genius and talents. And it is this fulfilling vision that alerts us to our particular purpose, an imagined goal that organizes our intelligence and lights our fire for the action to achieve it. So start the journey by thinking through your future image with the help of Exercise 11, "Future Image," on pages 161–162.

EXERCISE 11   *Future Image*

1. What would you like to be an expert in or famous for?

2. Imagine that you are to be honored and introduced to thousands. Write what you would like to be said.

3. What is your mission or purpose in life? What would you like to accomplish for others to remember you by?

    List your compelling forces—   List your constraining forces—
    your strengths for gaining this: your negatives and your weaknesses:
    •   •
    •   •
    •   •
    •   •
    •   •

4. What future actions are necessary for you to take to activate this mission or purpose?

5. What *actions* can you begin to take *now?* (Be specific.)

6. What can be completed in a month? One year?

E X E R C I S E   1 1   *Future Image (cont'd)*

7. Draw a picture of yourself (artistic ability is not the point, a stick picture is fine). Write a detailed description of your life and work today.

8. Visualize and describe yourself in detail five years from now. Where do you live? What are you doing in a typical day for work and leisure? Where do you work? Describe your appearance. How are you dressed? With whom do you communicate and on what subjects? What are you enjoying the most?

CHAPTER NINE

Free Agents and Entrepreneurs

Shake off your inertia and boredom—move out of your comfort zone.
Listen to your heart—know and act from your aptitudes and passion!
Start and learn along the way, never look backward. Three years ago, no
one would have hired me to do what I do now. True, I've spent eighteen
hours a day for three years, but I've never had more fun.

—Todd Wagner, CEO, Broadcast.com

The womb-to-tomb, up-the-corporate-ladder routine is long gone
for most people. And in spite of the rash of downsizing and all
the "early out" options, this is still a good time to be designing a
new career. However, it requires turning loose your former
guidelines and rules and recreating your work life. Current corporate paring ultimately will create opportunities for older workers if they keep on a sharp learning curve for their skills and pursue a "can-do" spirit. For the twenty-first century, consider
becoming a free agent or entrepreneur.

Taking an Independent Approach to Designing a New Career

In the early nineteenth century, 80 percent of Americans were self-employed, but this number fell to 9 percent by 1970. It is up to 10 percent, or twelve million small businesses, excluding farmers, and predicted to grow to 15 percent by 2000 and 25 percent by 2020. The U.S. contingency workforce has grown 57 percent since 1980, to approximately forty-five million temporary, self-employed, part-timers, and consultants. This contingency labor force—so named by the Conference Board, the world's leading business organization—is composed of workers who do not have a continuous employment history. These types of jobs are made to order for retirees who want to work some and supplement their income but have flexibility.

The contingency jobs available to retirees will be increasingly professional and flexible, and 51 percent of older workers plan to work part-time. Data from the Hudson study (Judy and D'Amiro, 1997) suggest that this contingency workforce could be one-fourth of the labor force by 2020, and 82 percent of the independent contractors prefer this. This group also includes 4.7 million professionals, such as lawyers and engineers.

How realistic is it to think older workers will get these contingency jobs? At New York–based IMCOR, Inc., nearly half of the three hundred to four hundred annual placements go to workers over fifty-five (Wright, 1997). According to John Challenger of Challenger, Gray & Christmas, Inc., International, "Unretirees—older workers, many who retired and then returned to work—are in great demand because of their depth of experience, extensive business contacts, and strong work ethic" (Challenger, 1998, p. 9).

One of my clients, an engineer with years of high-level international experience in a large oil company, was abruptly pushed into retirement. Ironically, this happened at a time when massive international opportunities were opening up in the Russian oil fields. Bob, whose parents were Russian, spoke the language fluently and knew the culture intimately. No one in his organization put this all together and said, "This man is a gold mine for us right now!" They focused instead on his chronological age and paid him to leave, creating in him initially a deep sense of loss and confusion.

With a little "free agent" thinking, Bob was able to design a new career by seizing on the rapidly emerging need for engineering consultants capable of dealing with the Russians. Bob connected with several consulting firms and is now a much-in-demand professional independent contractor making trips to Russia and working on his own terms.

Daniel Pink (1998) says there are 14 million self-employed Americans, 8.3 million who are independent contractors and 2.3 million who find work each day through temporary agencies. The IRS will mail out more than seventy-four million copies of Form 1099-MISC—the pay-stub of free agents. Adding them up, we end up with more than 16 percent of the U.S. workforce, which roughly rounds out to 25 million free agents in the United States, people who move from project to project and who work on their own, sometimes for months, sometimes for days.

Pink stresses that successful free agents are more invigorated and paradoxically more secure: "It's not only more interesting to have six clients instead of one boss, it also may be safer" (p. 132). The fundamental belief that we give loyalty in exchange for security has been shattered. Free agents know this and aren't wasting valuable time or energy bemoaning the loss. They realize that in the traditional work world they were accepting customs that should have crumbled years ago, and now they themselves must think about who they are and what they want to do with their life. Freedom means knowing your options.

Tom Peters takes a different twist, but recommends the same "free agent" style. He advises becoming a free agent or "a brand called you," in which he says we all have the choice to stand out—to win, learn, improve, and build up skills. But we have to know our distinctive brand. Regardless of where we work, independently or in an organization, "if you're really smart, you figure out what it takes to create a distinctive role for yourself—you create a message and a strategy to promote the *"Brand You"* (Peters, 1997, p. 86). You don't belong to any company for life, and your chief affiliation isn't to any particular "function." You are not tied to your job title or job description!

Ask yourself critical questions. What is my product or service? How is it different and superior to others? What have you done that you are really proud of and you can take credit for? Know your uniqueness and your value to your clients, customers, and employees.

The following is a model I developed for taking creative control of your career by marketing yourself. It applies to free agents in a job search with an organization as well as to professional independent contractors, consultants, and entrepreneurs developing a business.

- *Know your product thoroughly.* Know your strengths, uniqueness, accomplishments, success criteria, payoff, and purpose.

- *Believe in your product.* Maintain self-confidence, trust your abilities, competencies, creativity, and creations.

- *Research.* Who will pay you? Who needs your talents?

- *Develop and refine your selling tools.* These include marketing collateral, business cards, resumes, cover letters, job hunting, contacting, interviewing, and sales strategies.

- *Make the sale, negotiate terms, and close the deal.* Demonstrate how you would do the job. Communicate value for work. Ask for it; know you deserve and can do it.

- *Develop short- and long-term action plans.* Maintain a career contingency plan; keep learning and adding product knowledge.

- *Celebrate your successes.* Buid your self-esteem. Track current and future trends and learn from failures—keep learning till your last breath.

Consider Becoming an Entrepreneur

Sometimes the next move after working through the career change process is to move into entrepreneurship. The Entrepreneurial Research Consortium (ERC), made up of twenty-seven universities, surveyed what percentage of American households include someone who has started, tried out, or helped fund a small business. They anticipated the answer would be 10 percent, and some thought it might be as high as 25 percent. Researchers were stunned, however, when the answer showed to be 37 percent. In other words, more than one out of three American households is involved in entrepreneurship. "New and small businesses are a far more integral part of American life than anyone anticipated," according to Paul Reynolds, the ERC coordinator, a professor at Babson College at Wellesley (cited in Hopkins, 1997, p. 11). Entrepreneurship has arrived; entrepreneurs are the creators of the new economy.

The *Trend Letter* ("Building on a Prayer," 1998) reports that the number of small businesses in the U.S. has grown 57 percent, to about twenty-three million, since 1982. The major trend is from industry to upstart! Over six million U.S. households, or 6 percent of the total, have home-based businesses. They predict there is no stopping the entrepreneurial explosion. Small businesses are the driving force of the new economy, creating two out of three new jobs. Ours is becoming an age of innovation coupled with self-determination. It seems that most everyone is beginning to want to be his or her own boss and make his or her own decisions about when and how to do just about everything.

Economist William Dunkelberg, a Temple University professor, surveys the sixty-thousand-member firm of the National Association of Independent Business every month and has developed an accurate system for forecasting the total economy. According to current results, hiring plans are the highest in twenty-five years; plans to raise prices are low; capital spending plans are high; and inventories are solid and plans to add to them are strong (Associated Press, 1997b).

Several years ago, when Marge became a client, she had a degree in computer science, and for nineteen years she held responsible manager/supervisor positions in a large oil company. After her manager and long-time mentor retired, her work life changed dramatically. Her new manager ignored her and, without any real explanation, passed her over for two promotions. Over a period of time, we worked through job issues, and she succeeded in gaining her two promotions. However, by that time, she had decided to leave. She listed her greatest barriers to overcome as (1) the initial fear of leaving the first familiar company after so many years, though it had become painful; and (2) regaining the self-confidence eroded by her last manager's negative view of her professional contributions.

Marge's goal from the beginning was to become an independent entrepreneur, though earlier she had opted for organizational security. Her husband, an engineer, was talented and successful in this independent role himself, and though it seemed a distant dream, this became her long-term goal. She went back to school for an MBA to hone her business skills. She then became senior manager at a small (125 people) product development software company, which she left after hitting a glass ceiling.

She then partnered with a friend's husband who had a legal imaging business, and she opened a successful additional office—a very entrepreneurial endeavor—her ideal goal stated years before. The company has now been bought by a much larger organization, and she is to stay for the transition and perhaps longer. She is now thinking about her next step. Marge states in her evaluation that she feels a strong commitment to the environment of a smaller company, and she most enjoys the "experience of the small start-up company environment."

Marge's new career path did not happen easily, but was an ever-moving process. She believes that moving out of her box and connecting more with others earlier in her career would have helped her, and she feels her life would be "terrible" had she not made the career change. She has gained "new confidence in my innate ability," and states that she made a "major career realignment." Her advice to someone making a career change: "Look for something you really like." Marge represents the flood of women taking the free agent entrepreneurial route to career success.

For people thinking of starting their own business, Isachsen's *Joining the Entrepreneurial Elite* (1996), which uses the *Myers-Briggs Type Indicator®* personality inventory as a base, is a thoughtful resource. Another resource is *Entrepreneurial Style and Success Indicator* (1988), by Anderson and Shenson. Exercise 12 on the following five pages is a "Free Agent/Entrepreneur Characteristic Indicator" that I have developed from my work with entrepreneurs and from the literature. It provides some indicators to gauge the independent characteristic traits of adult clients.

However, I am most cautious in labeling individuals as having or not having entrepreneurial characteristics for the following reasons: first, these traits can evolve with circumstances. Adults can work with an organization for years but then break loose when they begin to see opportunities being dropped or

EXERCISE 12   *Free Agent / Entrepreneur Characteristics Indicator*

Indicate how true the following statements are about you by writing the appropriate number in the blank by each statement, using the following scale:

Not at All	Slightly	Somewhat	Quite Well	Completely
1	2	3	4	5

1. Need to feel a strong sense of control over my own destiny. _____

2. Have good health and a high energy level. _____

3. Set clear goals that are challenging and obtainable. _____

4. Have foresight and commitment to work toward these long-term future goals. _____

5. Have a firm belief in my ability to achieve my goals. _____

6. See myself as an overcomer with a high level of tenacity and determination. _____

7. Have moderate people skills and communicate well. _____

8. Stay relatively cheerful, cooperative, and tactful. _____

9. Impose my own standards and compete with myself. _____

10. Know how to build on successes and learn from failures. _____

11. Like situations where I can make a measurable impact. _____

12. Tolerate frustration and ambiguity. _____

13. Deal successfully with modest to high levels of uncertainty and job insecurity. _____

14. Can work on a number of different projects and issues at once. _____

15. Stay cool under fire and solve problems well under pressure. _____

16. See myself as fairly original and creative as well as analytical and realistic. _____

17. Seek aid from outside resources as needed. _____

18. Have the knowledge and/or technical skills in my field for building a business. _____

19. Understand the language of business, i.e., the financial and legal requirements, etc. _____

EXERCISE 12   *(cont'd)*

Not at All	Slightly	Somewhat	Quite Well	Completely
1	2	3	4	5

20. Have a healthy respect for making and managing money. ____

21. Have a close family member who has owned his or her own business. ____

22. Know I can do my work better than anyone else. ____

23. Tend not to be interested in outside investments over which I have no control. ____

24. Have a clear vision—a purpose—a plan to create and implement. ____

25. Not particularly interested in partnerships. ____

26. Willing to learn new skills to be more successful. ____

27. Not especially interested in managing or supervising others. ____

28. Have a tendency to focus on my own interests and concerns. ____

29. People tend to label me a workaholic since I appear to have limited outside interests. ____

30. Take only calculated risks, though others tend to see me as a risk taker. ____

31. Creating/designing a successful business is my major motivation. ____

32. Buying an existing business and building it is a major motivation for me. ____

33. Making money is an important measure, but not the only measure, of my success. ____

34. The approval of others is not particularly important to me. ____

35. Fear becoming stale in my work. ____

36. Making something out of nothing is a major motivation of mine. ____

37. Primarily motivated to do something very well. ____

38. Do not fit in a conventional, traditional organization. ____

39. Have a knack for spotting new ideas, concepts, and coming needs. ____

E X E R C I S E   1 2   *(cont'd)*

Not at All	Slightly	Somewhat	Quite Well	Completely
1	2	3	4	5

40. Constantly aiming higher than where I am currently comfortable. ____

41. Set realistic, attainable goals for my work. ____

42. My goals are consistent with my interests, values, motivations, and skills. ____

43. Compete with my past achievements rather than with another person. ____

44. Can delay gratification and work toward distant goals. ____

45. Can deal with temporary failure and mistakes on my way to my goals. ____

46. Have a "right" sense of timing, an instinct for the best time to act. ____

47. Practice continuous and increasingly ambitious goal setting. ____

48. Have the ego strength to know and admit when I'm wrong. ____

49. Consumed by my work since I find it stimulating, satisfying, and revitalizing. ____

50. Have high confidence in my abilities and competencies in my work. ____

51. Prepare well and leave little to luck or fate. ____

52. Except for business reasons, I am not a joiner by nature. ____

53. Have an ego that tells me "I will do well," not "I'm the greatest ever!" ____

54. Can master challenges, overcome obstacles, and realize my goals. ____

55. Can make a decision and act quickly. ____

56. Have difficulty working for others. ____

57. Know my weaknesses, and either overcome them or work around them. ____

58. Have faith in my abilities and skills. ____

59. See mistakes as temporary barriers and know that I will recover. ____

EXERCISE 12 *(cont'd)*

Not at All	Slightly	Somewhat	Quite Well	Completely
1	2	3	4	5

60. Take responsibility for my failures. ____

61. Can give great attention to detail if it's critical to my business. ____

62. Can balance facts and intuitive decision making. ____

63. Rely on my hunches and intuition for business decisions. ____

64. Can tolerate uncertainty. ____

65. Have always liked to make money. ____

66. Personal achievement and challenging work have always been important to me. ____

67. If I won the lottery, I would continue to work much as I do now. ____

68. Even when young, I was the leader, in charge, the one in control. ____

69. Control over my time and choices is important to me. ____

70. Have an instinct and history of turning negatives into positives. ____

71. Have little patience with game playing and office politics. ____

72. Thrive on responsibility and accountability. ____

73. Competitive by nature. ____

74. Fear failure, but that doesn't stop me. ____

75. Tend to work at odd hours when the mood hits. ____

76. Frequently find it easier to do things myself than to show others. ____

77. Become bored with a profession or business role after about two years. ____

78. Tend to be a perfectionist in my work product or service. ____

79. Use a good idea regardless of its source. ____

80. Want to pursue my life in my own way. ____

81. See corporate organizational life as restrictive, irrational, and intrusive. ____

82. Want flexibility to set my own pace, schedule, lifestyle, and work habits. ____

EXERCISE 12 *(cont'd)*

Not at All	Slightly	Somewhat	Quite Well	Completely
1	2	3	4	5

83. Hedge my bets. ____

84. Willing to lower my standard of living for future opportunity. ____

85. Don't rest on my laurels, but move on to another challenge. ____

86. Have sometimes felt displaced, disengaged, or a misfit in my work life. ____

87. Had distant relationship with my father. ____

88.   Mother was dominant but supportive of me. ____

89. Labeled nonconforming and rebellious by many others. ____

90. Had real problems dealing with authority figures in the workplace. ____

91. Have no problem doing things differently from others. ____

92. Feel as if I "march to a different drummer." ____

93. Have felt victimized by a former employer. ____

94. Many see me as having a killer instinct. ____

95. Feel confident I could succeed in many kinds of businesses. ____

96. Rarely trust outside consultants—especially counselors and academicians. ____

97. My biggest problems relate to personnel. ____

98. Don't do things by the book. ____

99. Always feel a need to keep learning. ____

100. Have a strong realistic, commonsense quality. ____

TOTAL ____

Range = 100–500. According to the literature and to CDA experience, the higher your score on the indicator, the more traits you probably have in common with free agents, entrepreneurs, or PICCs (Professional Independent Contractor or Consultant).

lost, or they know how it could and should be done differently. Feeling displaced and realizing that the system or policies will not change, they break away to do it themselves, and their entrepreneurial traits can grow dramatically. There are some, however, who have always been independent, have never worked in a corporate setting, and have long displayed the independent thinking characteristic of entrepreneurship.

Another reason for caution in a rigid definition of entrepreneurship characteristics is that women and minorities in the U.S. are currently starting businesses at a much higher rate. The research of the past on entrepreneurial characteristics may be most appropriate to white males. Another reason for my uncertainty in labeling entrepreneurial characteristics is that opportunities in the work world are moving away from manufacturing to services and knowledge. This may attract the kinds of people capable of and attracted to service work rather than manufacturing. Certainly the start-up costs in service businesses are not as prohibitive.

Also, many go independent in their work because they realize their opportunities for what they want to accomplish are limited if they work for someone else. In the 1960s, during my child-rearing sabbatical, I read an upbeat report that if a woman had a doctorate and was an achiever, she could have an excellent chance of becoming a college president. That became my aspiration. However, since the realities of family and teaching were demanding, it was the mid-1970s when I completed the degree and was ready to launch into the career path to become a college president. The reality of the times had changed, and while I was a dean in a small college that closed, it was evident that a Ph.D. would lead to no more than part-time teaching on a community college campus or at a second- or third-rate college—not goals I cherished. Entering the traditional corporate world at my age at that time, if an option, was not suitable for my temperament. My long-expected goal had vanished. It became abundantly clear that if I were to be president of anything and stay in charge of my own life, I would have to create it myself—which I did. I was forced to become assertively independent in the 1970s, as are millions of people today. And many of them are loving it as I have. Freedom is indeed knowing your options, which is my company credo.

Common Characteristics of the Entrepreneur

The following are some important characteristics for today's entrepreneurs.

Control. Control, not over others, but over his or her own destiny, options, schedule, and quality of product or service is probably the most compelling need of the entrepreneur. Highly individualistic, entrepreneurs want the freedom and options to do their own thing in their own way. Frequently displaced and disengaged, a small bit of control from others creates worries of confidence—they simply don't fit in someone else's system. They have been fired or left voluntarily to make a better product or provide an improved service.

Creativity/curiosity. These characteristics seem to be the universal need of baby boomers who ask: "What will I do with my creativity?" They are prime candidates for entrepreneurship. Entrepreneurs are innovative pattern makers, not pattern followers. The drive for the entrepreneur to create something from nothing is expressed in the sentiment "I want to create through my own efforts," and is tied to the need to build or create something that they *own.* Like the artist, their creation is an extension of themselves for the outer world to view.

Entrepreneurs seem comfortable in what appears to be chaos to others. They can change directions if they see the opportunity for a higher level of achievement. They can handle the lack of structure, improvise, invent, and improve along the way.

Competency. The ability to create perfection in product or service is very important to entrepreneurs. They are confident they can do something better than anyone else, and they stay on a learning curve about their product or service from any sources. Their need for perfection is as strong as their need for control. This perfectionism and the need for control and action create ambiguity—what I have labeled a "go, go/no, no" syndrome, which can be very confusing to managers and employees. They also seem to have the unique ability to see the forest and the trees simultaneously—that is, they can see the concept or vision clearly, and also the immediate steps for moving toward this future image. Both dreamers and doers, they act on the steps to create change.

Challenge/competition/consistency. High energy and drive for achievement are characteristic of entrepreneurs. They have a rising sense of aspirations, an unending sense of urgency to achieve something. Inactivity makes them restless and usually impatient, and they do not wait around well. They have a high energy level and the desire and tendency to set self-imposed standards that are high yet realistic and then to compete with themselves and their former level of achievement.

They are highly motivated by a challenge that they perceive to be interesting but not overwhelming. They are educated, calculated risk takers, and though it may appear they play for high stakes, they hedge their bets. Risk and entrepreneurs seem directly associated, yet entrepreneurs are not gamblers. They act only after they are convinced there is little risk.

They are persistent and realistic, make sense of complexity, and are confident in the face of adversity; these traits seem to make them "fail-safe" where others would drop off. They do not accept luck, fate, and so on as a third party in controlling their life; they disdain fatalism. They are consistently focused and constant in their pursuit of the goals they have set. They are not like Sisyphus, a trapped victim in a dreadful fate. When told that something can't be done, they ask, "Why not?"

Confidence. The successful entrepreneur almost never considers failure a real possibility. The self-confidence ("I'm going to do well") they exhibit is based on their anticipation, or belief, that they can and will successfully master challenges, overcome obstacles and barriers, and realize their wishes and desires. It suggests a strong ego, but not necessarily a power-driven ego like the big talker/poor listener.

Failure to most must be used as a means of gaining a better understanding of how to prevent the same thing from happening again. Most successful entrepreneurs have had at least one failure in their background, but are confident they will succeed this time. They are extremely self-confident and at their best in the face of adversity. When starting, building, or running their own business, they also often seem disease resistant—good health is a common trait of entrepreneurs, which is important because work can be relentless.

Courage and integrity. These qualities are evident in most successful entrepreneurs. They are not game-playing, clever, political, corporate guerrillas. They expect and accept statements to be true, and expect others to take their statements at face value also. They are realistic, but also idealistic. Sometimes they are blindsided by people who say one thing and mean something else. Entrepreneurs are usually trusting and not overly suspicious in their dealings with others.

Common sense. This quality enables entrepreneurs to deal with contradictions, uncertainties, and ambiguities in a tough-minded, optimistic, and realistic way. In a free enterprise system, opportunities are spawned in circumstances of change, chaos, confusion, inconsistency, lags and leads, knowledge, information gaps, and a variety of other vacuums in the industry or market. Entrepreneurs with credibility, creativity, and decisiveness can seize an opportunity while others merely study it.

Entrepreneurs are capable of dealing successfully with the problems and uncertainties of creating and running a successful enterprise. Theirs is not the optimism that is dashed by the first hurdle they hit. They know well that some you win and some you lose, but they plan on winning. Responsible and pulled by their vision and hopes for their future, they take action. Creating a business is a venture into the unknown and is the action of Maslow's self-actualizing person.

Commitment. The determination to complete a project once undertaken, regardless of conditions or frustrations, is an important characteristic for entrepreneurs. For some, career displacement with seemingly no other options is important in honing their commitment. Essential to success is a strong determination to get the job done at almost any cost in terms of personal sacrifice, and they view adversity as merely part of the pattern. It is important for the owner/operator to have the ability to set clear goals and objectives that are high and challenging, and at the same time realistic and attainable. There must be a commitment to long-term future projects and to working toward goals that might be quite distant.

Because of this commitment to their enterprise, successful entrepreneurs, though interested in making money, may well have a low need for status symbols. Their status needs are met by the achievement of their business, to which they are so strongly committed. The really successful entrepreneurs find their satisfaction in what it takes to build the business, not in appearances to others. Office decor, clothes, and the cars they drive are not so important to them. Symbols of position are not critical, and they can lower their standard of living to keep their commitment.

Communication. The ability to communicate ideas to others is vital in every business but imperative in the small business. Entrepreneurs need to be able to sell their business venture and themselves. Cheerfulness, cooperation, and tact are all-important. Verbal and written comprehension, and written communication ability are necessary for the entrepreneur.

Ed is an example of an adult in his second midlife who took the entrepreneurial risk route and did extremely well. He became a client about two years after he took early retirement. He had been a technical writer and editor for a large computer company for more than twenty years. He made a fantastic salary and enjoyed all the benefits that went with it. By most accounts, he seemed to be living the American dream. But things aren't always as they seem.

"I just wasn't happy doing what I was doing," said Ed. "But I was reluctant to leave my job and do something else." When his company began downsizing and started offering nice severance packages to employees as a way of cutting costs, Ed saw an opportunity to do something else with his life. "I wasn't completely sure what I wanted to do, but I had always had an interest in cooking." After doing a lot of research on some of the best culinary schools in the country, he finally decided to spend three months at a school in New York. "It was one of the best things I have ever done," said Ed, "but after it was all over, I decided that, while I did enjoy cooking, I didn't want to do it all the time. So I was faced with the question, "'Now what?'" That's when Ed became a client; we worked for six months. His dream was to integrate his talent for editing and his love of food. Ed had a talent for asking for business and taking action; based on this he started two businesses: a freelance editing company and a culinary newsletter. His services always seem to be in demand. He is really happy now, though he says that "running your own business is tough, no doubt about that. But I'm very satisfied with what I'm doing now." Ed has a well-planned home office, and is indeed a free agent.

Summary

While being a free agent, a PICC, or an entrepreneur has many advantages, it also has equally critical problems. However, as my clients have verbalized, it's apples and oranges—you simply prefer the oranges—you choose the problems to solve. As one female client, a successful partner in a large law firm working sixty to seventy hours per week, said after she went independent and opened her own practice, "You trade one set of problems for another, but at least you get to decide on the problems."

The Achilles' heal of the entrepreneur can be:

- Language: not speaking the language of the accountant, lawyer, etc.

- Regulated environment that requires much attention

- Facade/substance: losing sight of their purpose and direction

- As they get heavily committed, forgetting that a business is people

- Not having and using a timely financial report and not having the information needed

- Not being flexible enough to juggle all the roles. The small business owner must be chief executive officer, accountant, treasurer, lawyer, personal manager, production supervisor, marketing specialist, advertising agent, etc. No wonder tens of thousands of businesses fail each year.

Don't go the independent or entrepreneurial route unless you can feel passionate about what you are doing, and I don't use the term *passionate* loosely!

To successfully design a new career in your second midlife requires that you take active steps to move from the stereotypical view of older workers. However, in many cases, ageism can be diminished or overcome with a conscious and skillful self-marketing and sales strategy on the part of the worker.

If you plan to work in an organization, to get beyond ageism in the workplace you'll have to demonstrate that you have a strong work ethic; the willingness, energy, and good health to work hard; and no plans to retire. Show that you have the ability to work well both in team situations and independently, excellent interpersonal and communication skills, and the ability to adapt to the changing work environment. Gain new technical skills and/or continuing education experiences in the field. Older employees must be able to translate this experience into what the marketplace and the employer want and need, and what will add value.

Epilogue

We are not "senior citizens" or "golden agers" we are the elders,
the experienced ones; we are maturing, growing adults responsible
for the survival of our society. We are not wrinkled babies, succumbing
to trivial, purposeless waste of our years and our time.

—Maggie Kuhn

Just as there is no automatic system to successfully guide our
career for us, there is no prescription for how we are to live our
later life. Society and its institutions and professionals are trail-
ing at least ten years behind in dealing with the process and
problems of integrating aging and working.

Those of us who are embarking on our first or second midlife
are asking ourselves some critical questions: What is the purpose
of our later years? Does aging have any intrinsic purpose? Is there
work to be done after rearing children? What are the rules, rights,
and responsibilities of older people? What are the strengths and

virtues of old age? What is a good old age? Who can teach us how to grow old well? How can we deal best with time? Can we expect new thresholds to cross as long as we live?

In order to live successfully, we must believe in that for which we live. We become "old" when our belief system is gone, regardless of our chronological age. The most meaningful thing we can live for is to reach our full potential. We must find and develop the skills we enjoy using and pursue a positive idea of aging. And we must keep on a growth and learning curve.

We need to develop our own positive visions and purpose for our later life. It won't be given to us by our culture; we may get no more than a hint. In the past, we looked outward and surveyed. We accepted decisions without much questioning, confident that the future would be more of the same, a continuing model. We know now, or are rapidly learning, that this is not the case. We cannot rely on a changeless external environment. Our certainties must be generated from our own internal base, propelled by our own personal success criteria, rather than from relying on a particular condition of the outer work. This is wisdom in action.

As we move to the twenty-first century, from the brawn to the brainware era, a new breed, the free agent who can adapt and deal creatively with complexity and change, will thrive. To make this 180-degree shift at midlife, many must radically rethink their current beliefs about how to age and work. The following list is a summary of important power points for finding a new way to work in the twenty-first century.

- Know what you want, know that you deserve it, and know how to ask for it effectively.

- Find your purpose and passion and pursue them.

- Focus on active, functional aging by gaining insight into a new concept of time and aging and forgetting rigid chronological passive age.

- Know that understanding yourself and your purpose will anchor you in this age of uncertainty.

- Stay optimistic and maintain a sense of humor—age is much more a state of mind than a number of years.

- Realize that life and work satisfaction based on meaning and motivation is a major factor in increasing longevity.

- Understand that you will likely be living a longer, healthier life than previous generations, and that you need to make the most of these extra vital years.

- See the aging process as a positive time of continuing growth and ascent, focusing on our emerging freedom, options, and choices rather than the current popular image of decline, disarray, and decay.

- View aging, career, and lifestyle threads that you can creatively and consciously weave together in a pattern of your own design.

- Know that a stale, declining career spilling over into your personal life will leave you feeling old and stagnant, regardless of chronological age.

- Avoid the "victim" mentality and stay in control of your life as long as possible.

- Arm yourself with your own unique set of written success criteria for building your work and life.

- See a time of chaos and complexity as a time for renewal and rebirth: seek out the underlying order.

- Identify and discard the myths of aging, half-truths from an earlier age that disrupt and distracts from our career.

- Distinguish your "glass balls," which cannot be dropped without lasting, permanent damage, from the countless "rubber balls," which are only clutter.

- Constantly ask meaningful and thoughtful "grail questions" to seek and sort out what is really happening in your life and in the world.

- See aging and career planning as a continuing lifetime process.

- Develop latent, dormant characteristics and skills.

- View crisis as an opportunity for you and your family to refocus and move on.

- Realize that ageism is similar to racism and sexism, and the accompanying outdated aging myths, misinformation, and the resulting negative effects frequently are instrumental in turning older adults into mindless children.

- Recognize that you have options and choices for aging successfully. Practice becoming adaptable, alert, and active now and you will grow old that way.

- Know that the creative spirit, far from declining with age, may actually gain in strength and vigor if you concentrate on doing what really matters to you.

- Value and cultivate wisdom—the greatest gift of the human life cycle.

- Believe strongly in that for which you live—the greatest anti-aging secret.

- Be aware that dissatisfaction with retirement can accelerate the aging process.

- Live long—die fast. We will have an additional twenty, even thirty healthy years: we will be "old-old" for a shorter period of time.

- Remember that biological age responds to psychological age. For example, *longevity studies reveal that job satisfaction is the most reliable indicator of low risk for heart attack.*

- Understand that staying youthful is not about staying chronologically young. The pursuit of youth blinds us to the possibilities of age.

- Realize that aging is a lifetime "work in progress": we learn how to grow older just as we learned how to grow up.

- Know that the sense of community—the rootedness, belonging, and satisfaction we get from work we enjoy and where we live—is absolutely essential at any age.

- Be authentic: make your real self the same person inside as outside.

- Trust your instincts: beware the tyranny of conventional authority.

- Confront the fear of aging.

- Reject the negative aging stereotypes and paradigms that are pervasive, expected, and accepted today.

- Strive for robust aging, going beyond our current and normal "diseased" aging.

- Keep in mind that when self-esteem is high we seek success, and when it is low we seek to avoid failure.

Jung assures us that aging has purpose: "A human being would certainly not grow to be seventy or eighty years old if this longevity had no meaning to the species to which he belongs. The afternoon of human life must have a significance of its own and cannot be merely a pitiful appendage of life's morning" (1933, p. 109).

McLeish (1994b) summarizes the journey in late life:

The Ulyssean Sonnet

Naked of funds and power, I now consign
All my disasters to oblivion.
All the mischoices that I once called mine
I now resolve never to think upon.

What can I do that will undo the past?
I can review it, mourn it, waste my powers,
Replay the games no whistle can recast,
Try to relive the unrelivable hours.

No—at an age when fools say all is ending
I consecrate myself to fresh tomorrows,
Resume the Ulyssean Way I see extending
Its noble hopes beyond all sins and sorrows.

I take the Sacred Present and conspire
To ring the future with Empyrean fire.

Anderson, J. R. L. *The Ulysses Factor: The Exploring Instinct in Man.* Orlando, Fla.: Harcourt Brace, 1970.

Anderson, T., and Shenson, H. *Entrepreneurial Style and Success Indicator.* Clearbrook, B.C.: Consulting Resource Group International, 1988.

Associated Press. "Telecommuters Say They'd Walk Before Going Back to the Office." *Dallas Morning News,* Oct. 22, 1997.

Baltes, P. B., and Smith, J. "Toward a Psychology of Wisdom and Its Ontogenesis." In R. J. Sternberg (Ed.), *Wisdom: Its Nature, Origin and Development.* New York: Cambridge University Press, 1990.

Barker, L. "Molly Bogen Interview." *Dallas Morning News,* June 22, 1996.

Barker, L. "Take Charge Attitude May Extend Life." *Dallas Morning News,* Nov. 18, 1997.

Birren, J. E. "Creativity, Productivity, and Potentials of the Senior Scholar." *Gerontology & Geriatrics Education, 11,* Jan./Feb. 1990.

Birren, J. E., and Schaie, K. W. (Eds.). *Handbook of the Psychology of Aging.* (3rd ed.) Orlando, Fla.: Academic Press, 1990.

Birren, J. E., and Schaie, K. W. (Eds.). *Handbook of the Psychology of Aging.* (4th ed.) Orlando, Fla.: Academic Press, 1996.

Birren, J. E., and Schroots, J. E. "History, Concepts, and Theory in the Psychology of Aging." In J. E. Birren and K. W. Schaie (Eds.), *Handbook of the Psychology of Aging.* (4th ed.) Orlando, Fla.: Academic Press, 1996.

Bischof, L. J. *Adult Psychology.* New York: HarperCollins, 1969.

Bortz, W. M. *We Live Too Long and Die Too Short.* New York: Bantam Books, 1991.

"Building on a Prayer, Working on Faith." *Trend Letter,* Feb. 19, 1998.

Cetron, M., and Davies, O. "Extended Life Spans: Are You Ready to Live to 120 or More?" *Futurist,* Apr. 1998.

Challenger, J. "Workers in High Demand." *Futurist,* Mar. 1998.

Charness, N., and Bosman, E. "Human Factors and Design for Older Adults." In J. E. Birren and K. W. Schaie (Eds.), *Handbook of the Psychology of Aging.* (3rd ed.) Orlando, Fla.: Academic Press, 1990.

Chen, V. "Scattered Thoughts." *Dallas Morning News,* Aug. 4, 1997.

Chopra, D. *Ageless Body, Timeless Mind.* New York: Harmony Books, 1993.

Cole, T. *The Journey of Life: A Cultural History of Aging in America.* New York: Cambridge University Press, 1992.

Cole, T., and Winkler, M. G. (Eds.). *Oxford Book of Aging.* New York: Oxford University Press, 1994.

Comfort, A. *A Good Age.* New York: Crown, 1976.

Comfort, A. "Senility: Is It Mostly a Self-Fulfilling Prophecy?" *Brain/Mind Bulletin, 6,* Jan. 26, 1981.

Craig, J. L. "Old Age, New Attitude." *Menninger Perspective,* no. 1, 1996.

"Depression in Later Years." *New England Journal of Medicine, 3* (15), Nov. 18, 1997.

"Discovering Career Options." An interview with Dr. John Holland on the *Self-Directed Search.* Garland, Tex.: Career Design Associates, Inc., 1985.

Dossey, L. *Healing Words: The Power of Prayer and the Practice of Medicine.* San Francisco: Harper San Francisco, 1995.

Drucker, P. F. *Managing in a Time of Great Change.* New York: Truman Talley Books/Dutton, 1995.

Dychtwald, K. "New Image of Aging." *Brain/Mind Bulletin, 4,* Aug. 20, 1979.

Dyson, E. *Release 2.0: A Design for Living in the Digital Age.* New York: Broadway Books, 1997.

Einstein, A. Letter to Otto Juliusberger (September 29, 1942). Einstein Archive: 33–41.

Elias, M. "Aging and Memory: When to Worry About Forgetting." *Harvard Health Newsletter, 17* (9), July 1992.

Erikson, E. H., Erikson, J. M., and Kivnick, H. Q. *Vital Involvement in Old Age: The Experience of Old Age in Our Time.* New York: Norton, 1986.

Fackelmann, K. "Stroke Rescue: Can Cells Injected into the Brain Reverse Paralysis?" *Science News, 154,* Aug. 22, 1998.

Fagg, L. W. *The Becoming of Time: Integrating Physical and Religious Time.* Atlanta, Ga.: Scholars Press, 1995.

Ferguson, M. "The Transformation of Values and Vocation." In M. Ray and A. Rinzler (Eds.), *The New Paradigm of Business.* New York: Putnam, 1993.

Fossel, M. *Reversing Human Aging.* New York: Morrow, 1996.

Fox, M. *The Reinvention of Work: A New Vision of Livelihood for Our Time.* San Francisco: Harper San Francisco, 1994.

Freud, S. "On Psychotherapy" (1904). *Collected Papers.* New York: Basic Books, 1959.

Friedan, B. *Fountain of Age.* New York: Simon & Schuster, 1993.

Greider, K. "Making Our Minds Last a Lifetime." *Psychology Today,* Nov./Dec. 1996.

Hadnot, I. J. "Searching for Deeper Truths." *Dallas Morning News,* Dec. 18, 1997.

Harkness, H. *The Career Chase: Taking Creative Control in a Chaotic Age.* Palo Alto, Calif.: Davies-Black, 1997.

Harris, L. *Aging in the Eighties: America in Transition.* Washington, D.C.: National Council on Aging, 1981.

Hayflick, L. *How and Why We Age.* New York: Ballantine, 1994.

"Health News." *New England Journal of Medicine, 3* (15), Nov. 19, 1997.

Henry, S. "Keep Your Brain Fit for Life." *Parade,* Mar. 17, 1996.

Holland, J. *Making Vocational Choices.* (3rd ed.) Odessa, Fla.: Psychological Assessment Resources, 1997.

Homer. *The Odyssey.* Translated by Robert Fagles, introduction and notes by Bernard Knox. New York: Penguin Group, 1996.

Hopkins, M. "Gallup Survey: Americans at Work." *Inc. Magazine,* State of Small Business Issue, 1997.

Hoppe, C. "Lady Bird Invests in the Future." *Dallas Morning News,* Dec. 23, 1997.

Hopson, J. L. "A Love Affair with the Brain: A Conversation with Marion Diamond." *New Age Journal,* Aug. 1984.

Hultsch, D., and Devon, R. A. "Learning and Memory in Aging." In J. E. Birren and K. W. Schaie (Eds.), *Handbook of the Psychology of Aging.* (3rd ed.) Orlando, Fla.: Academic Press, 1990.

Isachsen, O. *Joining the Entrepreneurial Elite: Four Styles to Business Success.* Palo Alto, Calif.: Davies-Black, 1996.

"It's Not Over Yet: Ray Charles Interview." *Dallas Morning News,* June 9, 1997.

"Jack Nicholson Interview." *Dallas Morning News,* Nov. 18, 1997.

Judy, R. W., and D'Amiro, C. *Workforce 2020: Work and Workers in the Twenty-first Century.* Indianapolis: Hudson Institute, 1997.

Jung, C. G. *Modern Man in Search of a Soul.* Orlando, Fla.: Harcourt Brace, 1933.

Jung, C. G. "The Soul and Death in Psychology and the Occult" (1934). In *The Collected Works of C. G. Jung,* vol. 20. Princeton, N.J.: Princeton University Press, 1977.

Kanin, G. *It Takes a Long Time to Become Young.* Garden City, N.Y.: Doubleday, 1978.

Kaye, S. D., with Lord, M., and Sherrid, P. "Stop Working? Not Boomers." *U.S. News & World Report,* June 12, 1995.

"Keep Walking: Keep Living." *Harvard Health Newsletter, 23* (6), Apr. 1998.

"Keeping Your Brain Active." *San Jose Mercury News,* Apr. 23, 1997.

Kovar, M. G., and LaCroix, A. Z. "Aging in the Eighties: Ability to Perform Work Related Activities." National Center for Health Statistics Advance Data, 1987.

LaCroix, S. "Myth of the Shrinking Brain." *Intuition,* July/Aug. 1997.

Lehman, H. *Age and Achievement.* Princeton, N.J.: Princeton University Press, 1953.

Leider, R. "You Decide: Work and Life: Are You Deciding on Purpose?" *Fast Company,* Feb./Mar. 1998.

Levin, J., and Levin, W. C. *Ageism: Prejudice and Discrimination Against the Elderly.* Belmont, Calif.: Wadsworth, 1981.

Livermore, B. "Build a Better Brain." *Psychology Today,* Sept./Oct. 1992.

"Looking Ahead: Implications of the Present." *Harvard Business Review,* Sept./Oct. 1997.

McLeish, J. A. B. *The Ulyssean Adult: Creativity in the Middle and Later Years.* Toronto: McGraw-Hill Ryerson, 1976.

McLeish, J. A. B. *The Challenge of Aging.* Toronto: The Ulyssean Society, 1994a.

McLeish, J. A. B. "The Ulyssean Sonnet," from *The Far Shore Dimly Seen.* Toronto: Studio High Techniques, 1994b.

McRae, H. *The World in 2020: Power, Culture, and Prosperity.* Boston: Harvard Business School Press, 1994.

Moore, T. J. *Lifespan: Who Lives Longer—and Why.* New York: Simon & Schuster, 1993.

Neugarten, B. (Ed.). *Middle Age and Aging.* Chicago: University of Chicago Press, 1986.

New York Times News Service. "Genes Key to Intellect of Elderly." *Dallas Morning News,* June 9, 1997a.

New York Times News Service. "30% Pick Death over Nursing Homes." *Dallas Morning News,* Aug. 6, 1997b.

Nuland, S. B. *How We Die.* New York: Knopf, 1994.

Nuland, S. B. *Wisdom of the Body.* New York: Knopf, 1998.

O'Hara-Devereaux, M., and Johansen, R. *Global Work: Bridging Distance, Culture, and Time.* San Francisco: Jossey-Bass, 1994.

Oxford English Dictionary. (2nd ed., vol. xx) Oxford, England: Clarendon Press, 1989.

Perls, T. T. "The Oldest Old." *Scientific American,* 1995.

Peters, T. "Brand You, Inc." *Fast Company,* Aug./Sept. 1997.

"Preventing Alzheimer's Disease." *Johns Hopkins Medical Letter,* June 1997.

Restak, R. M. *Older and Wiser: How to Maintain Peak Mental Ability for as Long as You Live.* New York: Simon & Schuster, 1997.

Russell, C. *The Master Trend: How the Baby Boom Generation Is Remaking America.* New York: Plenum, 1993.

Ruth, J-E., and Coleman, P. "Personality and Aging: Coping and Management of Self in Later Life." In J. E. Birren and K. W. Schaie (Eds.), *Handbook of the Psychology of Aging.* (4th ed.) Orlando, Fla.: Academic Press, 1996.

Ryder, N. B. "The Cohort as a Concept in the Study of Social Change." *American Sociological Review, 30,* 1965.

Salthouse, T. A., and Maurer, T. T. "Aging, Job Performance, and Career Development." In J. E. Birren and K. W. Schaie (Eds.), *Handbook of the Psychology of Aging.* (4th ed.) Orlando, Fla.: Academic Press, 1996.

Sapolsky, R. M. *Stress, the Aging Brain, and the Mechanisms of Neuron Death.* Cambridge, Mass.: MIT Press, 1992.

Sarason, S. B. *Work, Aging, and Social Change.* New York: Free Press, 1977.

Schaie, K. W. "Intellectual Development in Adulthood." In J. E. Birren and K. W. Schaie (Eds.), *Handbook of the Psychology of Aging.* (4th ed.) Orlando, Fla.: Academic Press, 1996.

Scheibel, A. "Structural and Functional Changes in the Aging Brain." In J. E. Birren and K. W. Schaie (Eds.), *Handbook of the Psychology of Aging.* (4th ed.) Orlando, Fla.: Academic Press, 1996.

Schmidt, F. L., and Hunter, J. E. "Joint Relation of Experience and Ability with Job Performance." *Journal of Applied Psychology, 73,* 1988.

Schrof, J. M. "Brain Power." *U.S. News & World Report,* Nov. 18, 1994.

Senge, P. "Communities of Leaders and Learners." *Harvard Business Review,* Sept./Oct. 1997.

"Sex May Prolong Life." *Mind/Body Health Newsletter, 7* (1), 1998.

Sheehy, G. *Understanding Men's Passages.* New York: Random House, 1998.

Simonton, D. "Creativity and Wisdom in Aging." In J. E. Birren and K. W. Schaie (Eds.), *Handbook of the Psychology of Aging.* (3rd ed.) Orlando, Fla.: Academic Press, 1990.

Spirduso, W. "Age Shouldn't Keep You from Trying a New Sport." *Dallas Morning News,* Aug. 8, 1997.

Spirduso, W., and MacRae, P. "Motor Performance and Aging." In J. E. Birren and K. W. Schaie (Eds.), *Handbook of the Psychology of Aging.* (3rd ed.) Orlando, Fla.: Academic Press, 1990.

Stern, C. "Depression Is a Silent Killer." *Parade,* Sept. 28, 1997.

Sternberg, R. J. (Ed.). *Wisdom: Its Nature, Origin and Development.* New York: Cambridge University Press, 1990.

Taves, M. J., and Hansen, G. D. "Seventeen Hundred Elderly Citizens." In A. M. Rose (Ed.), *Aging in Minnesota.* Minneapolis: University of Minnesota Press, 1963.

Taylor, R. A. "How I Flunked Retirement" (interview with Lee Iacocca). *Fortune,* June 24, 1996.

Thurow, L. C. *The Future of Capitalism: How Today's Economic Forces Shape Tomorrow's World.* New York: Morrow, 1996.

Vaillant, G. E. *Adaptation of Life.* New York: Little, Brown, 1977.

"We Are Not Lone Wolves." *Mind/Body Health Newsletter, 7* (1), 1998.

White, K. "How the Mind Ages." *Psychology Today, 26* (6), Nov./Dec. 1993.

Wolman, B. B. (Ed.). *Handbook of General Psychology.* Englewood Cliffs, N.J.: Prentice Hall, 1973.

Wright, J. "Job Picture for Older Workers Brightens." *Dallas Morning News,* July 20, 1997.